Dear Barbara!

Thank you for
your support of Vehicles

Much
love

Janet

Keep

GAIL

Climbing

MacDONALD

TYNDALE HOUSE
PUBLISHERS, INC.
WHEATON, ILLINOIS

ACKNOWLEDGMENTS
While this book may show the name of one author,
it has been a team effort. The support I have
received through prayer, notes, and phone calls
from my friends, especially Jan Carlberg, Shirley
Clemmer, Lowell Sykes, Keith and Judy Fred-
rickson, Virginia Friesen, Ruth Wessel, Robyne
Bryant, Miriam Hayes, and Lois Wells, will always
remain in my grateful memory. The encouragement and competence of my editor, Dawn Sund-
quist, spurred me on. Not only did she treat the
manuscript with much care, but her attention to
detail and her expertise in writing have caught
errors and given added understanding to certain
passages.

Beyond them, of course, has been the consistent cheerleading I have received from Gordon,
Mark and Patty, and Tom and Kris. May each of
you find some small encouragement in knowing
you have played a major role in the completion of
this book.

Cover photos by Gordon MacDonald

Library of Congress Catalog Card Number 89-50619
ISBN 0-8423-2036-9
Copyright 1989 by Gail MacDonald
Printed in the United States of America

3 4 5 6 7 8 9 10 95 94 93 92 91 90 89

To GORDON,
my climbing partner
of twenty-eight years:
Together we have
loved the peaks;
Together we have lived
through the valley.
Together we will see
The best is yet to be.

CONTENTS

FOREWORD

I married the author of *Keep Climbing* twenty-eight years ago. I love her and like her more today than I ever have before. So then, you would not be surprised if I recommended this book without reservation and, at the invitation of the publisher, gratefully write its foreword.

Another reason for my enthusiastic endorsement would have something to do with the fact that I shared the climbing experience about which Gail writes. In fact, I was the one who suggested the route, not realizing that we were taking on something a bit more ambitious than an afternoon's promenade in the park. Frankly, I wasn't prepared to admit my blameworthiness for that choice when we hit some of the rough spots that day on the walk to the top, but I'm comfortable with taking responsibility now that our serendipitous adventure in the Swiss Alps has become a marvelous and positive memory.

As in the case of our "walk" to the Strela Pass, I have

probably been the instigator of most of the climbs we've made at other times when the purpose was something more than recreation. I was the one, for example, who proposed that we take our newborn son and move to the Kansas prairie and live as a young pastor and wife among hard-working farming families—a culture we admired but knew nothing about. I can still visualize Gail working outside in the dead of a vicious winter to unfreeze the vertical shaft of a frozen windmill that pumped our water from the ground. And I can see her cautiously stalking a rattlesnake with her trusty hoe so that our toddler would not be harmed.

I was the one who a few years later suggested that we make the southern Midwest our home and serve a congregation that had been badly bruised by conflict. And I can visualize Gail decorating our home and receiving literally hundreds of guests for dinner during the time we were there as we tried in our own way to teach love and reconciliation through servanthood. I also remember her exhaustion after having taken one too many phone calls from someone else in trouble who needed a word of stabilization. Even Gail has a few faults, I suppose, and one of them is not knowing when to quit. That "quality of fault" would be fortunately revealed once again on the day about which she writes in *Keep Climbing*.

Again, I was the one who thought that Gail would adjust easily to a New England congregation and told her so. And she did when we moved there. My memory contains a picture I saw many times when I peeked in the rear door of the church sanctuary on Tuesday mornings and listened to her teach the Bible to several hundred women. My memory also retains the sights and sounds of a home in which our two teenagers, Mark and Kris, felt free to invite their friends for meals and conversations of which Gail was often the center. I see her cheering wildly on the sidelines for both of them when they competed in sports. In fact, I see that same loyalty as she silently cheers for me each Sunday when I preach the gospel of Christ.

You would suspect that I was the one who planned the itinerary of a thousand (or so it seems) trips back and forth across the country and sometimes the continents asking Gail to acclimate to new situations with people of all ages, cultures, and spiritual status. And on every occasion as we made this life-climb together, I saw the life of God in her as she served with me, encouraged me, and lovingly told me truths I needed to hear and wouldn't have heard from other sources.

More recently, I asked Gail to join me in the high-rise apartment living of New York City, to face the challenge of urban life at its most intense, and to move among some of the most amazing people in the world who represent a score of races, cultures, and life-styles. And so here we are climbing again in a place God has set before us. We've gone from rattlesnakes to subway tokens; from windmills to fax machines; from farm coops to bagel shops; from ranchers to stockbrokers, diplomats, and the tragic homeless. And still Gail keeps climbing.

But I've only mentioned the mountain peaks and high meadows of our climb together. I also asked Gail to walk through valleys with me. I didn't mean to, and I would give anything if I could roll back history and delete the valley-choices from our itinerary. But life isn't like that, unfortunately. So the author of this book walked the valley with me, too. And, if on other days of our climb I had seen Christ-like qualities of toughness, adaptability, hospitality, motherhood, mentoring, and compassion, I saw in the valley other things in my partner: kindness, mercy, grace, and the determination to keep climbing.

Keep Climbing is built on the wonderful moments of one day in our lives together. But it is a metaphor of twenty-eight very special years. And every principle illustrated in this metaphor of the climb to the top works. I know because I have seen them firsthand in the life of the one who has written about them. A resilient and determined woman kept climbing that day, and she's been doing the same sort of thing every day we have climbed other mountains together. Perhaps now you can appreciate why *Keep Climbing* means so much to me.

GORDON MacDONALD
Fortunate husband of the author
Canterbury, New Hampshire, and New York City

INTRODUCTION

Astride the winding, narrow road from the city of Chur to
the city of Arosa in the Swiss canton of Graubunden is the
tiny village of Langwies. Langwies, population three hundred, has two small hotels, a bakery, and an almost miniature
Swiss Reformed church. At the bottom of a steep hill is the
village railroad station. Bright red narrow-gauge trains arrive
there seventeen minutes after every daytime hour, headed
toward Chur and thirty-three minutes after the hour, headed
toward Arosa. As with everything in Switzerland, the two
trains are always on time. Apart from the post office (called
the PTT in Switzerland), a school, and a modest collection
of Swiss chalets, there is nothing more to Langwies except
beauty. The town fairly drips with serenity and simplicity.

Several thousand feet above the village are vast mountain
meadows reached by single-lane dirt roads and footpaths.
There Swiss farming families live during the summer months,
cutting and raking the grasses that will provide winter feed

for their dairy herds. At the onset of the cold, the families leave their high-altitude chalets and drive their cows down to winter shelter in Langwies and other towns in the valley. Then the skiers take over the slopes the cows had earlier occupied.

Langwies captured our affections the first time my husband, Gordon, and I made a trip to Switzerland. We happened upon it as if by chance at that time of the day when travelers who have no itinerary begin to think about a place to sleep. We found a room at the Alte Post Hotel, and soon after check-in, it occurred to us that the country around Langwies might be excellent for walking.

Walking! Not ten-minute strolls in midafternoon, mind you, but long walks—walks that may be several hours and kilometers in duration and distance. Before we ever heard of Langwies, we had learned that the only way to really appreciate Switzerland is to see it on foot. Besides, walking is a national pastime for Europeans, and we, too, were easily swept up in its enjoyment.

The Switzerland we discovered on our walks is a country laced with paths called *wanderwegs*. Well maintained, excellently marked, and most not overly strenuous, they are ideal for people like this midlife couple who simply want to ramble from point to point, absorbing the breathtaking beauty of the Alpine scenery.

By the time we came to Langwies, we had already walked along the fast-moving, emerald green mountain streams that are colored by the rich limestone of the region. We had walked through French, Germanic, and Romansch villages, marveling at the Swiss penchant for neatness and cleanliness. And we'd seen some of the Swiss forests where each tree stands straight and tall in groves so perfectly farmed that you suspected each one was noted and monitored in a government computer until it was time to be harvested.

In Langwies we studied the map (the *wandercarte*) and

found a wanderweg that seemed ideal. It appeared to wind up the mountainside, pass through several small, summer alpine villages, follow an enlarging snow-fed stream, and then climb to a point called the Strela Pass. From the Strela, the map seemed to suggest, we would be high enough to have a spectacular view of an entirely different part of Switzerland. We could look down on the famous ski town of Davos and across to the Tyrolean Alps of Austria.

Maps can be deceptive to the inexperienced, and we were certainly among the inexperienced. No doubt that's why we concluded that a walk up the Strela Pass wanderweg would be a marvelous idea for our first long trek in the area; the route on the map appeared to be relatively easy. It would take about four hours to ascend and three to descend. We went to bed that night anticipating an early morning start.

It was during that walk the next day from Langwies to the Strela Pass that this book was born. For what Gordon and I discovered rather quickly was that we had undertaken more than a routine walk up a hillside. Serious mountain climbers would have considered the way to the Strela little more than a warm-up for bigger things, but we found ourselves facing something a bit more challenging than we had anticipated. I can now admit it: More than once during those hours, I wanted to turn back. But I didn't, and we kept climbing.

As I strained to take each step upward that day, I began to see that our physical attempt to reach the Strela Pass was not unlike another challenge, a spiritual one, that I was trying to meet. For the walk to the Strela Pass was parallel to a challenge that was going on in my inner being. An inner climb, if you please.

The inner climb was tied to my choice (made years ago) to follow Jesus through life no matter the direction, the roughness of the pathway, or the quality of the weather along the route. My resolve as his follower was to be like him as much as possible in personality, character, relationships, and decision making. Or to put it, more simply, in the words of St. Paul: "to be conformed to the likeness of his Son."[1] So if the goal of the outer climb was to reach the Strela, the goal of the inner climb was conformity to the likeness of Christ. To pursue the latter goal meant learning to trust that Christ was on the "climb" with me and that, no matter what happened, he would never abandon me. He never has.

More than one writer I have read has used the climbing of a mountain to illustrate truths about the spiritual life. Among them, no one has impressed me more than Amy Carmichael, who lived the last twenty years of her life with the results of a debilitating accident. Her inner climb of the spirit as she struggled to fulfill her sense of purpose from a sickbed was a remarkable feat. I'm sure she never would have chosen the painful pathway she was on for those twenty years. But choosing to accept the unexplained, she followed Jesus, pressed ahead, and kept climbing.

There are aspects of my climb in life that I would not have chosen either, but Carmichael's "climb," being much more arduous, became an inspiration to me. In fact, her words came to me as our walk toward the pass began to increase in unexpected difficulty. I heard her saying:

> *"Anything but that, Lord" had been your earnest prayer. And then, perhaps quite suddenly, you found your feet set on that way. Do you still hold fast to your faith that he makes your way perfect? It does not look perfect. It looks like a road that has lost its sense of direction; a broken road, a wandering road, a strange mistake. And yet, either it is perfect or all you have believed crumbles like a rope of sand in your hands. There is no middle choice between faith and despair. Life is a journey; it is a climb; it is also always a war!*[2]

Something of a stranger to mountain climbing or hiking before coming to Switzerland, I'd never fully appreciated why

word pictures like these were so important to Amy Carmichael. Now, as I climbed upward, her way of putting things
became clearer to me. For as I've already said, it would have
been easy to turn back if something within me had not been
convinced that perseverance until we reached our goal was
important.

Frankly, there were times on the inner climb when it might
have been easier to turn back also. But Carmichael made the
point clear: Life itself is a climb, even a battle; there is often
little choice between bold faith and crippling despair.

As I began to compare the inner and the outer climbs that
day above Langwies, everything seemed to take on significance and symbolic value to me: the tiny pool of water from
which we took refreshment; Gordon's hand, which steadied
me at a point where the rocks were wet and slippery; the
cable someone had long ago affixed to the side of a wall so
that walkers could feel secure as they traversed a dangerous
slope; the tiny patch of grass where we could stop, rest, and
restore ourselves before the final "rush to the top."

Some people seem to make the climbs of life in the easiest
possible way—up a cable car or ski lift. People with lots of
money can hire a helicopter. Others pick the easy trails. But
not a few of us reach the top the hard way, either by choice
or by circumstance.

I'm not sure I have much to say to those for whom life is
a cable car or helicopter ride. And I'm sure there are people
who have had to trek on trails much more difficult than the
one I have been walking for these first fifty years of my life.
But somewhere in the middle, between those who have had
it as easy as it can be and those who have suffered immeasur-
ably, you can find me. From this perspective, I have chosen
to write about a few themes that describe what has been
important in my climb in life.

The one who invites us to make each climb is none other
than the Son of God himself. For each of us, the inner wan-

derweg seems to be custom-made. On the way, there are scores of obstacles, and some of us apparently turn back. But for those intent on discovering what life at the top is all about, I have only one central piece of advice, which saturates every chapter of this book: *Keep climbing!*

GAIL MacDONALD
Canterbury, New Hampshire, and New York City

ONE
Walking with Purpose

The problem is not merely one of woman and career, woman and the home, woman and independence. It is more basically: how to remain whole in the midst of the distractions of life; how to remain balanced, no matter what centrifugal forces tend to pull one off center; how to remain strong, no matter what shocks come in at the periphery and tend to crack the hub of the wheel.
ANNE MORROW LINDBERGH

CHAPTER ONE
Why Are We Walking?

"Are you sure we know what we're getting ourselves into on this walk today?" That was the first thing I'd asked Gordon when I'd awakened that morning at the Alte Poste Hotel in Langwies.

"I've been studying the map again for the last few minutes, and I still think it looks terrific," he said. "I get the feeling you could probably jog to the top. The view up there has got to be unbelievable."

"So you're sure we're not taking on something too strenuous for us?"

"Not according to this map. Besides, we can check with the innkeeper at breakfast. She probably knows this countryside like the back of her hand."

So we asked her. "The Strela Pass? A nice walk," she said with a wave of her hand. "Three hours to the top at the most."

The day's destination had been chosen that easily. A cursory study of the map and the hometown appraisal of the innkeeper were the decisive factors for our decision, and after filling our backpacks, we started off. For a while on that beautiful morning, we had no reason to question what we had decided to do.

Why would anyone spend a lovely day in Switzerland walking? Why not, for example, purchase a Swiss Railway Holiday Card and ride trains from one end of the country to the other? Why not tour the big cities like Zurich, Berne, and Geneva in those magnificent European buses that look as if they are washed every thirty minutes? Why not ride the remarkable cable cars and cog trains that ascend a hundred Swiss mountains? Why? Because we had forged a mutual sense of purpose for this trip that was greater than simple sight-seeing or vacationing.

Our overarching purpose in going to Switzerland had been to renew our spirits, our minds, and our relationship. We had experienced the most difficult year of our lives, and we thought it necessary to break away from everything at home for a time and be alone. We wanted to do something that would stretch our minds and exercise our bodies. We were looking for the obscure places, the tiny things, the simple people, the grand vistas. And we would only find them, we'd decided, by walking together in those places that were far from the noises of the city and the bigness of the crowds.

So in accord with our purpose and its method, we had acquired the familiar short Swiss hiking pants, long, colorful socks, and backpacks. Then we'd asked questions of experienced walkers we met in various hotels and restaurants to see what they thought were the best places for novice walkers like us.

"Go to Arosa," some had said. "You will be sure to find there just what you want." And so we had, and Langwies— not far from Arosa—had been our stopping place.

All of this choice making, traveling, and question asking was purpose-driven, and now we were finally on one of those walks; our purpose in coming to Switzerland was being achieved.

I reminded myself of all this as we began to climb and I noticed my leg muscles were weakening. Whenever I begin to get tired in any circumstance, the first questions that come to mind are: Why am I doing this? What does it mean? And when will it be over?

It was natural for me to turn to these questions. For when anything in my life grows steep, I gain strength and determination by asking how this or that conforms to a purpose of some kind. Should I find that any activity in my world is not purpose-driven and plan-oriented, I am immediately involved in an inner struggle that doesn't stop until I've worked it through.

People who operate by purposes and plans usually make lists of things, and I am one of them. There are lists of action items I wish to get done at home. Lists of people I want to write. Lists of things to purchase at the markets. And lists of things I want to read and study. The lists are prioritized and formed into plans, then items are checked off, one by one, as I get them accomplished.

We plan-oriented people like such structure to our worlds. We feel at home with routines while serendipity is something we have to work at.

I have a husband who prefers to be just the opposite. He likes the unexpected and enjoys the challenge of thinking on his feet, facing unanticipated obstacles, and overcoming them with ingenuity. That may explain why, when we are driving somewhere, he'd rather guess at how to get there than stop and ask directions. In fact, I have been known to tease him about being like Erma Bombeck's husband, who also was apt to lengthen a short trip because he refused to ask for assistance. Erma once said to him, "Driving behind you is to see America first!" We have found it to be a great line to help us smile at our differences in temperament.

Although the two of us may differ in how we plan a trip somewhere, whether to a friend's house or to the top of Switzerland's Strela Pass, we have both come to strongly believe one thing: Behind all significant activity in life is the discipline of purpose. The older one becomes, or the greater one's pain or adversity in life, the more important the issue of purpose becomes.

It is not enough to ask, "What will I do today?" or "Where will I go?" These are action questions—good but not good enough. Actions should spring from purpose. And questions of purpose are usually more difficult. What will this decision mean? Why should I go here? Where will this pathway lead? What is the wisest use of my capacities, my experiences, my call from God? These are only sample inquiries, but I have come to believe one rarely asks enough of them.

If action questions need to be backed by purpose, so does another kind of question: the priority question. When I am among Christian women, one of the most frequently raised issues is that of sorting choices. "What's really important?" we like to ask one another. "What should I stop doing? What's the best thing to commit to?" But in each case, I'm inclined to argue that priorities, like actions, cannot be defined and sorted out until the big purpose question is asked and resolved.

Questions of purpose increase in importance not only with age or struggle but also with the number of things we have to do, the decisions we have to make, the people who make demands on us, the circle of our relationships, and our skills, spiritual gifts, and natural abilities. Purpose questions provide the foundation for the selections we make when it comes to determining when we will say yes and when we will say no.

As we age, we are more keenly aware that our days are indeed numbered and that we can only do so many things and know so many people. If there is not an underlying purpose to choices, those days and the elements of energy we have will probably end up being squandered.

This is what has driven me to the point where I see only one answer to such a concern: *Discipline life by the formulation of a purpose.* Harness life with such questions as: What are the truly important things God wants me to do with my years? Where will I seek to make my maximum contributions? And, what do I have to give out of the wealth of my good and bad experiences, my skills and gifts, my mind and spirit?

If I do not have answers to these questions, or if I have not formulated the answers so that I can measure each day by them, it is likely that my life will soon slip out of my control and into the hands of people and circumstances around me. As Gordon has noted in his book *Ordering Your Private World,* time and choices not submitted to purpose often become dominated by emergencies, weaknesses, people who intimidate, and superficial values.

I remember the day the importance of a purpose first came to me. Gordon, his staff associates, and the lay leadership of our church had been working on what they called a "Corporate Purpose" for the congregation. They were convinced that it was important to develop a simple statement that would become the focal point for all efforts in the congregation's life—a straightedge against which all activities could be measured. It would be a weekly reminder as to why we met and what we were supposed to be. I pondered what they were doing from a personal perspective.

Companies have corporate purposes, I said to myself. *Schools have statements of objectives. Military forces have missions. Why have I never formulated a formal statement of purpose for my life?*

When I asked that question out loud among my friends, they seemed surprised. "How can someone as busy as you say she has no purpose?" they asked.

Well, I argued back, I was sure I had a purpose behind everything I was doing. But the truth was that I had simply never identified and defined it, put it into writing, and consciously forced my daily planning through its parameters. If it seemed to be a good enough exercise for a church to do after years of existence, why wouldn't it be a helpful discipline for me? Furthermore, what I was thinking about seemed reasonable when I turned to Scripture.

Jesus was clearly purpose-oriented. He identified with the specific purposes set forth in Isaiah as he read them in the synagogue in Nazareth.

In another place, he noted that he had come "to seek and to save what was lost."[1] His focus was Calvary, an ever-present, weighty anticipation.

St. Paul was clearly aware of an overarching purpose to his life. He was out to develop mature, Christ-like people, he said. His hope was to dot the countryside with groups of followers of the Lord who would form congregations. No investment of energy was too great to make sure the maximum number of people heard about the cross and the love of Jesus.

Mary, the mother of our Lord, was very much aware of a purpose given to her by a heavenly messenger's call. Other biblical personalities also seem to show the signs of a life disciplined by a sense of purpose: Moses, Joseph, Ezra, and Esther, to name a few.

Purpose was important to these men and women because there were so many potential distractions to distort their values and their planning. As Jesus walked from place to place, he faced the pressures of what his disciples thought he ought to be making happen, what the crowds of people felt his agenda should be, and what the men of organized religion, the Pharisees, thought he should be saying and doing. Even Satan made a strong attempt to dissuade him from the direction in which he was walking. But all to no avail. Our Lord never caved in to outside influences. He had an all-pervasive purpose that was written deep within his inmost being; he reaffirmed it regularly before his Father and was unafraid to say no to those who tempted him to deviate from it.

If purpose was important in that ancient time, is it not a hundred times more important today? For now we live in a world that confronts us with more choices, more opportunities, more temptations than anyone ever knew in earlier times. Today we almost drown in our options and our pressures.

A friend returned to the United States after spending four years in a developing country. "What has been your biggest shock in reentering our culture?" I asked her.

"Walking down the potato chip aisle in the supermarket," she answered.

At first I laughed because on the surface her comment did not seem profound or insightful. But she went on.

"The potato chip aisle is symbolic of everything our family seems to be facing on this visit home. Four years ago when I went shopping, there were only a few brands and varieties of potato chips on the shelf from which to choose. But now when I head for that part of the store, I find I am faced with more choices than I have time for. Do I want potato chips that are plain or rippled, barbequed or flavored with sour cream and onion, with salt or without? I can have nacho cheese, jalapeño, or cheddar. It's unbelievable! I'm almost paralyzed by indecision. All I wanted was a simple little potato chip. *Why*, I ask myself, *should I spend important minutes in life deciding what kind of a potato chip I'm going to buy?*

"My friends aren't even aware of the energy it's taking, they've gotten so used to the subtle enslavement. So you ask me what has shocked me? It's seeing the time wasted over 'potato chip decisions,' so that when the truly important issues need our attention, our energies have already been squandered on trivia."

What a difference my friend's insight has made in my life. "Potato chip moments," I have begun calling them—those times when one gets inundated by insignificant choices and decisions. If we lack a perceived purpose, we are slowed to a crawl because we aren't sure what is truly important anymore.

But this matter of purpose is about more than just the purchase of products. It has to do with the allocation of our energies in schedules that often are excessive and exhausting. Most of us face unlimited opportunities every day—opportunities to learn, to do, to know, to experience.

At the same time we are trying to decide between our opportunities, we are bombarded by the persuasive voices of those who call to us for our time, our loyalties, and our resources. In spite of their oft noble objectives, the fact is that they usually attempt to seize the initiative in our lives before we do and before we have made any effort to discover what God is saying to us.

All of this can be like a good news/bad news joke. The good news is that we have all of this from which to choose; the bad news may be that we haven't much of an idea how to make mind-settling choices.

And so the issue, I think, is clear: Unless there is a strong sense of purpose lurking somewhere within us, we can expect our lives either to bang about like the ball in a pin-ball machine or to come under the control of those who are more than glad to create purposes for us.

When Beverly Sills was a child, she dreamed of being an opera star. Nevertheless, in spite of her fantasy of the future, she hated to practice. Each day her parents had to prod her toward her musical disciplines. One day, in exasperation, one of them said to her, "Beverly, you need to learn to like what you love." Sometimes you and I do not like what we say we love because we aren't clear enough about it in our definition of purpose and how that is to be fleshed out in our daily experience. Where these matters become fuzzy, less-than-best alternatives are likely to interfere.

When a purpose-driven person appears on the scene, one is likely to see certain admirable traits. We're talking of people who move through their day with an economy of action, people who seem to be aware of how to conserve their energy for the important issues. These are people who have planned the allocation of their time, and they know how to say many noes and when to say yes. Their living seems balanced, ordered, and targeted. They appear not to panic in the face of setbacks and frustration; they persevere in times of opposition; and they are not easily seduced or dissuaded by the flatterer or the critic. An idealistic portrait, I confess. But this general run of marks is more often than not present in purposeful people.

I was stimulated to do some important thinking one day when I picked up a book that presented the opinions of several wives of famous men. The author's specific agenda was to discover what purposeful living meant to these women who were married to men in the public eye.

One woman said that the only worthwhile pursuit she could think of was the acquisition of money. "Earning your own money is your identity." Another, the victim of a tragic divorce, said, "I never want to be in a supportive role again." But then sandwiched between such opinions was the answer of Mrs. Billy Graham. When asked what she would like to do with the last third of her life, Ruth responded, "Help Bill."

I was stimulated by the answer Mrs. Graham gave to the question that was addressed to her: What will you do with the rest of your life? I pointed the question at myself, and several resolves began to emerge slowly as I looked within and searched for the witness of God's hand upon my life. I discovered a couple of interesting things when I took something like a microscope to my life's performance.

I saw that for nearly thirty years I had worked from a "relational perspective"—the notion that relationships are the most important thing—and that this perspective was growing even more important to me as I grew older. Thus, any formal purpose statement for me would have to be built on the understanding that my relationship with God was the supreme priority. Second, it would have to reflect the importance of knowing myself as fully as possible. Third, it would have to be built on the significance of my relationship to my husband and my children. Beyond that, it would take into account a host of treasured friends, our congregation, and a world where I knew I was called to make some sort of contribution. But that relational order had been and always would be important.

As I looked backward, I saw that I am a home-oriented person, which means that I tend to enjoy living out my purpose in the place where we live. It's there that I can serve my loved ones most effectively and create an air of hospitality for those who come to visit. I like to think of myself as one who is striving to be a homemaker, a people-builder, a steward of things in whatever place people come together as family and friends.

If I cannot be at the locality we normally call home, then I find I instinctively try to make a home wherever I am: a hotel room, a tent in the wilderness on a canoe camping trip, a suite at a conference center where Gordon and I are speaking. I simply like the atmosphere of a home. A home should be the safest, the most peaceful, the most growth-oriented place in our lives. I find tremendous satisfaction when I am able to create pockets of safety and encouragement for those who are close to me at any given time. A place of grace, if you please.

Therefore, with thoughts like these in mind, I set out a few years ago to write a purpose statement for myself. I discovered that purposes do not come out of the blue. They reflect the voice of God in the inner spirit; they spring from a host of past experiences where we have known the pleasure of God through what we are and do. And, of course, purposes are partly shaped out of failures: knowing what doesn't work, realizing what God has not called us to, being sensitized to hurt and injustice.

A friend of mine had sought to define purpose for herself, and she did it far more simply and perhaps more profoundly than I have. "Choose life," she wrote as she put an entire life's purpose into two words. For her, that simple affirmation springing from the Book of Deuteronomy meant that whenever she had a choice to make, the life-giving solution was the one that would help her make up her mind.

"We can eat a candy bar or an apple," she said. "But which leads to a greater quality of health? We can watch TV or read a book. But which leads to a greater quality of growth? We can say the loving word or the critical word. But which conveys the quality of personal nourishment?" And so she chose to drive her purpose—the choice of vital, healthy, growth-oriented life—through every action in the day. Ultimately, of course, her dream is to help others choose life as well. Will they embrace life as Christ offers it or resist life and break themselves over his truth?

As I pursued the formulation of a formal statement of purpose, I found that my discipline of journaling became a great help. As I scanned back through the months, I was able to discern values and patterns of living through which the hand of God had been obvious. It was important to me that my purpose sprang from the Scriptures, so I began to scan them for someone whose life rang true to what I believed God was asking me to become, someone whose devotion to Christ would stretch me beyond where I was or ever dreamed I could be.

And I found her! *Mary of Bethany*—sister to Martha, sister to Lazarus, and friend to Jesus. A fascinating woman who understood perfectly how to make a difference whenever she was with Jesus and his friends. In the pages just ahead, I will want to talk about her in greater detail and why I found her to be such a personal inspiration.

Having found Mary of Bethany and a sense of compatibility with her life and perspective, my purpose statement began to take shape. Its content went through months of formation and reediting. But when I was reasonably sure that the simple sentences reflected what I heard God saying within, I typed it out and placed it in my notebook. Throughout the years, the wording has changed, but the essential focus and meaning have remained the same.

I do not share it with you because it deserves emulation either in form or in content. It simply serves as an example of what can be done when one determines that purpose is the place to begin the significant climbs in life.

> *I purpose, through the power of Christ within, to follow the example of Mary of Bethany who chose to set moods, be sensitive, and love sacrificially. Fully aware that my own growth is in process, taking a lifetime, I will live patiently, relax, and enjoy the journey.*

This purpose statement became my flag. Morning after morning, I would read it, affirm its grip upon my being, and then, in light of it, set out to write my lists of things to do that day, always asking how this or that item contributed to my sense of purpose. Frankly, the answers do not always come in the obvious sense. But the discipline is first, and the direction is set before the motion begins.

I wanted my purpose to center on my relationship to God and not on the approval of the crowds with their flippant opinions and loyalties. I wanted it to be durable so that, when defined, it need not change or diminish in significance if I passed through a momentary failure or grand setback. And I wished my purpose to give me a sense of fulfillment even if no one else saw value in what I was doing.

I purposed, for example, to give a major chunk of my life

to the development of two children, Mark and Kris. In concurrence with Gordon, I decided that income production was not as important as the character and maturation of two human beings we would hope to give to society. There were times when Gordon and I saw other couples doing things or investing in something that we found financially impossible because my purpose was not to add to our material resources. And there were times when I felt challenged or put down by those who thought that mothering as a vocation was a second-class way of life in our modern world.

It was my purpose, in part, that carried me through those temptations to envy or to feel less valuable than others. Now that we are enjoying the lives of Mark and Kris as adults, we are most grateful that we stuck to the purpose; it has been worth its weight in gold.

I am fully aware that thousands of women today would have chosen to give themselves fully to the development of their children, too, but circumstances beyond their control have prevented it. I realize I have been fortunate to have the opportunity to make such a choice.

Not long ago, Gordon and I led a retreat for a number of young company presidents and their spouses. In one of the evening sessions, we presented our personal purpose statements (my husband has written one, too) and why we thought they were important. The next morning as we once again convened, one of the men spoke up.

"I didn't sleep much last night," he said.

"What was the problem?"

"I was trying to write my personal purpose."

"And what did you learn?"

"I learned that it was not an easy thing to do. I've written corporate purpose statements for a dozen companies. But it hit me last night that I'd never thought about that exercise for myself. It makes a lot of sense. But it sure is difficult."

The pathway from Langwies to the Strela Pass began to

climb higher. Already, I was beginning to feel the first hints of fatigue. Were we sure that we wanted to exert this much energy? Could we make it to the top? Would it be worth it? What was going to keep us going?

Purpose, I suppose. There had to be some reason deep down that would keep us climbing. And indeed, there was. For we had come to Switzerland to experience the unusual, the beautiful, the restorative, the challenging. That was our purpose. And we were going to achieve it in part on the walk to the Strela. So instead of turning back when the going toughened up a bit, we kept climbing.

CHAPTER TWO
Keeper of the Moods

In the small packs we carry on our backs as we walk the winding, climbing path toward the Strela Pass are a small loaf of freshly baked bread and several pastries. It is tempting to want to stop and eat them all immediately.

When we left the hotel that morning, we had passed the *bakerei*, and it seemed wise to stop and purchase something that might make rest stops a bit more nourishing and enjoyable.

In that brief visit to the bakery, we made our first friends in Langwies. Hans-rudi, the baker, had been up since three o'clock, firing his wood-burning oven and laying out the ingredients for the breads, buns, and assorted bakery goods that people of the valley would come to buy during the day. Norma, his wife, was behind the counter when we walked through the door to make our purchases. She was unusually cheerful and spoke English, and we were quickly conversing with her about life in a small European village like Langwies.

Since that first encounter, Hans-rudi and Norma have permitted us to enter a part of their lives, and we have returned to Langwies for further visits. On each of those occasions, we've learned more and more about the traditional life of the Swiss village baker.

Why does a young man rise at such early hours six days a week? What motivates him to work as long as sixteen hours each day for a relatively modest income? And what does his wife, Norma, gain from a life-style in which work virtually consumes the best part of every day?

As we came to know Hans-rudi and Norma, we quickly learned that they were purpose-driven also. Hans-rudi saw his role in the community as far more significant than the mere baking of a "two-kilo" loaf of dark bread.

"The people of the valley can get along without meat," he once said to us in his German-accented English. "They can live without milk and other dairy products, and they can forgo their vegetables for a while. But the one thing every Swiss family needs every day is bread. I must have the bread ready each morning."

The people of Langwies clearly appreciate the baker's importance—so much so that for more than a century a plot of Alpine pasture has been set aside for any cows he might wish to graze. Land in Switzerland comes at a high premium, so this is a provision of great significance.

One particular day when we were in Langwies, Gordon spent several hours with Hans-rudi as he drove the bakery truck to neighboring villages in the valley. "It's important to be at each village at the same time each week," he told my husband. "And I must be the one who comes with the bread or the people will say, 'Where is the baker today?' They trust me to know exactly what they need. It would be upsetting to them if they did not see my face. Watch, and you will see for yourself: The older women will simply hand me their baskets and their purses. They know I'll put into their baskets what they need and take only the money that I need."

The baker, we learned, is sometimes the community chaplain. "Many times, I will see a man or a woman linger behind the rest of those who have come to buy my bread. I know what is probably going to happen. They want to talk about a family problem or a personal matter that they do not feel they can even share with the pastor. They think I'll understand. After all, I'm the baker, and I know about everybody's problems. I never talk about what I hear. They are sure I'll keep their secrets."

When we ask Norma and Hans-rudi if they could ever come to America and visit us in our New Hampshire home, they shake their heads. "Perhaps in twenty years," Norma says. "But now we could not leave the bakery. The people of the valley need us too much, and there is no one to take our place for so many days."

This is a couple who lives by a purpose—one that far exceeds running a bakery business or selling the maximum number of breads. It marks their marriage; it dominates their choices; it says much about their sense of significance in life. I am challenged by their dedication to the people of their valley.

When I began developing my purpose statement, it occurred to me that I needed to let two important principles guide me. First, the purpose should match the things I saw in the Bible as being of eternal significance. Second, it must be practical, not a lovely-sounding statement that would only be read, admired, and then put on the shelf and permitted to fall into disuse.

It didn't take me long to identify on both accounts with a poignant event in the lives of Jesus and the woman, Mary of Bethany, whom I mentioned earlier. It happened in Mary's hometown where she, her sister Martha, and their brother Lazarus—all personal friends of Jesus—lived. The Apostle John informs us that six days before the final Passover in our

Lord's earthly life, Jesus came to visit with his friends. Following the Sabbath day's rest, a feast was held in his honor.[1] Mark, who also relates a version of those events, tells us that the dinner occurred in the home of a man known as Simon the Leper.

As far as we know, about fifteen people were present, and Mary and Martha appear to have been the only women in the group. While others seemed to have been there to eat and visit, Mary obviously had another idea: Worship!

Mary is a remarkable lady. Each time we see her in the Gospels, she is either listening at the feet of Jesus or finding a way to get there. On this occasion, we are told that, using a costly, sweet-smelling perfume and her hair, she wiped and soothed the feet of Jesus. Bible scholars say the unbinding of a woman's hair and its use as a towel was a mark of great humiliation, a presentation of personal honor to Jesus. One gets the feeling that Mary had thoughtfully chosen to pull out all the stops to show her gratitude and admiration for the Lord.

In this special act of servanthood, Mary did at least three things about which I feel strongly. The first of those was this: *Mary set a new mood* in that room of men. She was so intent on what she did that it appears she was oblivious as to what anyone else thought about her actions. Her objective was to honor the Lord, and if that offended the opinions and favors of others, it did not matter. He alone was the object of her sacrifice and worship, not other people. What's more, she didn't nag or try to force others to join her in what she did. Mary was acting on behalf of herself. Much to the surprise of those who began to criticize her, Jesus affirmed her actions.

One moment the room had been filled with the conversation of men dining and having a good time. No doubt there was laughter, an exchange of a memory or two, perhaps a moment of intensity as they pondered the implications of the threats they were hearing from their adversaries. It is a typical portrait of friends enjoying time together. A rather nice mood, I think. But there is a better one on the way.

Under Mary's direction, something that might otherwise have been light and convivial was properly repositioned toward something more serious. For when Mary broke open a container of extremely valuable perfume and used it in such an unusual way, pouring it on the feet of the Lord, she quickly got the attention of all. At her initiation, the mood became very somber—and rightfully so.

A female distinctive through the ages has been the ability to intensify or diminish, direct or redirect the moods of others. I cannot explain it, but I am aware that women have a subtle persuasiveness when it comes to mood setting. They possess a "leverage" that can move others to higher—or lower—ground. Women can choose to use this persuasiveness as Eve did, to derail good intentions, or, as Esther did, to redeem bad situations.

I've met more than a few women who do not like to admit that they have this mood setting capacity. Perhaps in denying it, they seek a strange sort of parity with men. Or perhaps in denying it, they seek an escape from the responsibility of it. I think they fool themselves.

In saying this, I am not hinting at some sort of seductive, Mata Hari-like female power. But, as the saying goes, I know it when I see it—an influence that can alter or establish a powerful mood in people. And it is an influence that usually belongs to a woman.

Whether or not Mary was conscious that what she was doing was setting a mood, I do not know. I only know that she accomplished just that. She forced the table conversation and the attitudes of men to change.

Gordon has often referred to me as the "emotional pendulum" of our home. He used to remind me frequently that he and the children (when they were young) often picked up whatever mood I was projecting. All three of them, he reflected, instinctively monitored my mood as they came through the door after a long day at work or school. If I was cheery and enthusiastic, they soon caught the mood. And if I was in another sort of mood, one that was less desirable, it usually set the direction for them also.

Some could be offended by Gordon's point. Some could say that too much responsibility was being placed upon my shoulders. And I can think of a few times when I was indeed tired of the responsibility, too.

But on the other hand, if it is true that our family most often tuned its moods to mine in the same way an orchestra tunes its instruments to the pitch of the oboe before a concert begins, then perhaps I should embrace this reality gladly as part of my purpose. A heavy responsibility, yes. But also a privilege.

That is why I came to love what someone said about the English mother of Bishop Moule: "Her feet brought light into a room."

Or the comment of a North African about Lilias Trotter, a gifted artist turned missionary who spent her life serving and enjoying the Algerian people: "She was still and created stillness. She is beautiful to feel near. I love the quiet of her."

Most of us know about John Wesley, who in the eighteenth century founded Methodism, but we probably know relatively little about his hymn-writing brother, Charles. Professor David Lyle Jeffrey, in a biographical account of Charles Wesley, says of him:

> . . . his spiritual character was luminous, and communicated itself immediately to those who came into conversation with him. William Wilberforce . . . was captivated by Charles. He met him in 1786 in the house of Hannah More, and his later recollection of that encounter reveals something of the special presence of this unusual man: ". . . when I came into the room Charles Wesley rose from the table, and

coming forward to me, gave me solemnly his blessing. I was scarcely ever more affected. Such was the effect of his manner and appearance that it altogether overset me, and I burst into tears, unable to restrain myself."[2]

Charles, like the bishop's mother and Lilias Trotter, was clearly a mood setter. And these two people of the past possess a quality of spirit that I would like to have in the execution of my purpose.

Abigail of the Older Testament was a mood setter for King David at one of the low points in his life. The young man had been running and hiding from Saul for quite some time. Then he received news that the prophet Samuel, his dear friend and mentor, had died. These events, spread out over long months, no doubt had taken their toll on his resolve.

For some time, David had offered protection and assistance to a wealthy sheepman whose name was Nabal. Now at a later, difficult time, David sent men to ask Nabal if he might reciprocate the earlier favor of food and shelter. But they were abruptly refused and insulted.

Of Nabal and his wife Abigail, the Bible says, "She was an intelligent and beautiful woman, but her husband, a Calebite, was surly and mean in his dealings."[3]

When David heard of the insulting way his men had been treated, his response was decisive. "Put on your swords!" And taking four hundred men with him, he set out to avenge himself. It was clear: David was hopping mad.

But David never reached Nabal. Abigail intercepted him on the way. Refusing to reflect Nabal's nasty mood, she collected two hundred loaves of bread, large containers of wine, meat and fruits enough to feed an army, and went out to meet David. Skillfully, she persuaded him away from his murderous intentions.

Abigail pointed out David's peacelike style of the past and suggested this was no time to change. She affirmed his previous unwillingness to hurt those who had sought to hurt him. And then she encouraged him not to mark his conscience with a needless angry act; he had too great a future, she said, and revenge against Nabal wasn't worth the effort.

Obviously, David was impressed. Abigail seems to have understood exactly how to defuse David's temper and get him headed in a new direction. And David knew it.

> David said to Abigail, "Praise be to the LORD, the God of Israel, who has sent you today to meet me. May you be blessed for your good judgment and for keeping me from bloodshed this day and from avenging myself with my own hands. Otherwise, as surely as the LORD, the God of Israel, lives, who has kept me from harming you, if you had not come quickly to meet me, not one male belonging to Nabal would have been left alive by daybreak. . . . Go home in peace. I have heard your words and granted your request."[4]

Ten days later, Nabal was dead of an apparent heart attack.

This story seems to be a beautiful illustration of how we were meant to assist one another in weak moments. David was not by nature a killer. He had refused to kill Saul at other times when doing so would have been clearly an exercise in self-defense. But now in a vulnerable moment, all of his self-control seemed to have vanished, and he was ready to kill another man for much less significant reasons. A strange inconsistency.

But Abigail was the mood setter, the woman who knew exactly what to do in terms of the right words and the right actions. Look at what she accomplished. She saved Nabal's life for the moment. She saved the lives of his entire family. And she helped restrain David from making what might have been a major error of judgment that would negatively affect his future.

Abigail and Mary have been inspirations to me as I have

worked out what it means to set moods in my world. Many times I fail. But it is an important goal out in front of me each day.

We call our home on the hill in New Hampshire "Peace Ledge," and recently friends came to visit us there. It was clear when they arrived that they were exhausted, their inner resources seriously depleted. How could we make our home a haven for them while they were with us? How could we make it possible for them to be renewed? How could we pour restorative grace into their lives?

We began with the morning hour. A tray with fresh-squeezed orange juice (to simulate Florida), fresh-brewed coffee, and fresh flowers was waiting at their door when they awakened. Soothing music was playing on the stereo as our weary friends came downstairs. They sat for quite some time absorbing the order of our home and the serenity of the morning. Only a few feet away, birds outside were flitting back and forth from the feeder. The Scriptures were opened to a reassuring psalm.

It was a time for letting the guard down, for being oneself, for experiencing the feelings of being loved, accepted, and comforted. I watched my friends' tears begin to flow quietly— tears, perhaps, of stored-up hurt and bewilderment; tears of relief for being in a place where there was no danger of personal attack; tears that come when one experiences joy again in simple and beautiful things. A pocket of safety. We had prayed that Peace Ledge would always be a house of grace, and our prayer was being answered that morning.

In a home, mood setting may happen with the appropriate words, decor, orderliness, noise-control, and choices of ways to celebrate special moments. Among friends, it may have to do with carving out times and places where people can feel free to share joys as well as disappointments and difficult questions. Notes, gifts, or flowers (or even pretty weeds) carefully made or chosen and sent at a timely moment—these can have a remarkable effect in lifting people to higher ground.

I have noted, on many occasions, that moods are closely correlated to the establishment and maintenance of routines and commitments. Because I am one who loves routines, this theme is closely attached to my own sense of purpose. In our family, I have chosen the role of being the custodian of routines.

Routines and commitments seem to connect and stabilize people, and most of us, as a rule, are in our best operating moods when we feel connected and stabilized. In this world of constant change, routines seem to disappear very easily unless someone determines that a few important things will stay the same.

At Peace Ledge, Gordon and I have certain routines that mark virtually every day. We often laugh at our mutual habits, but we would grieve deeply to lose them. One routine—a rather colorless one, actually—has to do with drinking our first morning cup of decaffeinated coffee while we watch the six o'clock news. We watch the same newscast every morning, and we realized one day how routine-oriented we are when the network, with no comment whatsoever, replaced the newscaster with another and we found ourselves strangely upset. To this day we have no idea what happened to the person we had watched for so long or why she is gone. It was like the disappearance of a friend. So it took a certain amount of time to adjust to the change.

As we became acquainted with the people of Langwies, we became aware how important routines and commitments are for them. It made us realize how few routines are built into the community life of modern American towns or families. In Langwies, the church bells toll on the hour; the trains arrive promptly twice each hour without fail. You can set your watch by the arrival of the PTT man on his scooter delivering the mail.

WALKING WITH PURPOSE

In the longer perspective of routines, the cows will return to the valley from the Alpine meadows every autumn, driven down the mountainside by all the townsfolk; the men of the village will gather to repair the roads at the same time every spring; the young men will go off to their annual two-week military activity in the same season; and the women will insure that the annual village festival happens on the same day each year. These routines mark the times and the seasons and provide a kind of simple security of mind and mood that contributes to the wellness of life.

All right, I'll admit it: I love routine! And it's not hard for me to see that moods of life and feeling are best established when people know what to expect. So my purpose causes me to be a keeper of the routines in our family—mealtimes, as well as the traditional observances of birthdays, anniversaries, holy days, and important events in other's lives.

Maybe that's one of the reasons Luke the physician is my favorite Gospel writer. It's Luke, for instance, who often highlighted the simple routine of eating together. Jesus seemed to value and make the most of the times he took to be present to people at meals.

It takes lots of energy and not a little perseverance to accept responsibility for some semblance of routine in life. Especially if one prefers to live serendipitiously, like someone I'm very close to.

We first began to grasp the concept of routines and commitments during graduate school days. On one occasion, Gordon had promised a friend who pastored a small congregation of twenty-five people that he would preach for him at a Sunday worship service.

But as the weekend approached, we discovered we had a crisis on our hands. A deadline had come: We would have to vacate our apartment on Monday, and we were forty-eight hours in advance of that moment with no place to go. Sunday was the last possible day to look for an apartment, so the temptation was great to call the pastor and tell him we would have to break our commitment.

Of course, it would be a major inconvenience to him because he and his family planned to be away that Sunday. He'd have to disappoint them or find another person to preach. But we also had a great inconvenience on our hands. Wasn't it best to put our situation first?

No. We decided it wasn't. It was our normal routine to worship on the Lord's Day, and usually we were busy in some form of service—preaching, teaching, helping in the nursery, being with people. It didn't seem right to interrupt that routine even in the face of our perceived emergency. We had made this commitment to help another person. So we ignored our crisis for the moment and went on.

Little did we know in our going that among that small group was the answer to our prayers. After the service, I began to greet people. I had noted a woman sitting in a wheelchair who had a quadriplegic handicap. I was instantly drawn to her because she seemed a woman of cheer, a person who had obviously brought self-mastery to a very difficult life-style. After admiring her from a distance, I made my way over to greet her.

I was not disappointed. Immediately, she asked if Gordon and I could come to her home for dinner. I thanked her but declined. We had to grab a fast hamburger, I responded, because we had to find a place to live in the next few hours.

"You're kidding me," she said.

No, I informed her, I wasn't kidding.

"I may have the house you're looking for," she went on. She described a small home that her husband had just finished renovating. A house with a fenced-in backyard (we had a two-year-old boy and a puppy). A house with a piano they'd like to leave in it (both Gordon and I play but had had no room for a piano). A house near shopping facilities (we had one vehicle). A house that was affordable (they would match the rent to our fiscal limits). A house that had to come right from the hand of God and be delivered by a lady in a small congregation that we had been tempted to avoid.

That weekend we learned a powerful lesson and reaffirmed our "doctrine of the routine," which simply says: Do what you've prayerfully committed yourself to do, and let God vindicate your choice. Or, put another way, if you believe God has called you to certain convictions, certain responsibilities, certain relationships, maintain them first at all costs before you turn to the more glittering alternatives that seem to come out of the air. That's routine. That's commitment.

I look back on that incident, which happened almost twenty-five years ago, and realize now what I didn't fully appreciate then: I probably had held the key to our choice to do the right thing. As a mother with a small child, I could have belabored the issue that we were within twenty-four hours of losing our home—and driven my point home with justification. I would easily have gained Gordon's attention with an argument in favor of family responsibility: Finding a place to live was of greater importance than his preaching at that small church. But gratefully, God put it into my heart to encourage Gordon to follow through on our routines and commitments which eventuated not only in our keeping our word but in receiving a blessing from God that exceeded our fondest dreams. I never forgot that lesson and have drawn from its precedent many times since.

Part of being a mood setter meant that I assumed responsibility for keeping the routines alive in our family's life together. Especially difficult was the routine of eating our evening meal together. Church, school, and peer schedules all militated against it, but I was as insistent as I could be. Sometimes family members complained, and there were many times I would have liked to give in because it seemed tiring to be the bad guy.

Based on a recent article from 1987 *Trends Update* by the

Food Marketing Institute in Washington, D.C., only half of American families "always" eat together. Sam Smith, professor of animal and nutritional science at the University of New Hampshire, points out that:

> *Traditionally, dinner is a time when we used to transfer a lot of cultural values. These values are now picked up on television, from friends, out behind the barn, where they used to be transferred around the family dinner table. In losing the tradition of family meals, there's a whole variety of social and cultural values that we've lost.*[5]

Today the four of us look back on the family experiences built around eating together and are most thankful. It was at the dinner table that we learned to talk and spur each other on to thinking Christianly. The mood during eating was as important to me as what we ate. If, when the children were small, they came into the kitchen with a bad attitude, they were kindly asked (hopefully with humor) to leave the room and return only when they had a better attitude.

A nice tablecloth (to cut down on noise), fresh flowers or colorful weeds (to add life to the table), and candles (to make us all feel valued) added a dimension of surprise to each evening. Sometimes, when we were eating leftovers that looked ghastly, I would turn off all the lights and use only candlelight. I called it "Italy Night" (with apologies to all Italians)! I assumed that I could pull any menu over on the family if I called it an exotic Italian dish.

The mood in a home is positively affected when each member of a family feels loved, touched, heard, and appreciated. Is it a coincidence that, from the first hours after birth, the nursing mother of necessity will maximize eye contact and touch? Were we not created to need touch and someone to be there for us? Are we to suppose that this need changes with the years?

Supreme in the processes of touching is the experience of

affection. Charles Whitfield, in his book *Healing the Child Within*, says that touching has to be ranked among the most important of human needs. Whitfield, a University of Maryland psychiatrist, spends most of his time working with alcohol- and chemical-dependent people. He is also an authority on co-dependency and abusive treatment in the addictive family. From his vantage point, he affirms the opinion set forth by Virginia Satir that all of us need from four to twelve hugs a day as part of our health maintenance. A simple, and astounding, yet greatly underestimated necessity.[6]

Of course, one immediately wonders what Whitfield's and Satir's observations say about the scores of single people who, whether by choice or by circumstance, are usually starved for an affectionate touch. What of the many in marriages that have grown cold where touching rarely happens? Gordon and I are frequently impressed with the number of couples with whom we have visited where there is not the slightest hint of physical contact the entire time we are together.

Return to the story of Mary at the feet of Jesus. Her gentle ministrations toward his bruised and soiled feet were an act of gentleness and friendly affection. Some in the room were put off by her act. But Jesus was comforted.

Somewhere I heard the story of a group of young medical students who were training in a large pediatric ward of a teaching hospital. As time passed, it was observed that one student was particularly loved more than anyone else by the children. Someone set out to discover why.

The student was followed through his rounds for an entire day, and there seemed to be nothing exceptional about his performance. But in the evening, the mystery was solved. For as the lights were being turned out for the night in the various rooms, the student doctor managed to stop by the bedsides of all the children and give them a simple kiss good-night. He was setting the mood for their sleep hours. A pocket of safety.

What that physician seemed to be doing was exactly what

was so often on my mind when our children were young. I saw it as a major objective, a part of my purpose, that affection would overflow in our home. Affection, rightly used, would itself create a mood that would make each member of the family feel safe, appreciated, and motivated to grow. I could not find enough excuses to touch our children. Hugs, stolen kisses, backrubs, and hands held when walking were forms of affection we showered on our children in their youngest years.

When our children reached the teen years, I learned, like every other mother, that most adolescents are embarrassed by forthright affection from their parents. But there were ways to get around that. Being the mood setter, I would walk into a room and simply announce, "Mom has skin hunger." It was a signal that everyone in the family understood: I was approaching someone for a simple cheek to cheek touch. They laughed at their silly mom, thinking they were satisfying my spoken need. But deep inside, we both knew it was their need as well.

In a book by Megan Marshall, *The Cost of Loving: Woman and the New Fear of Intimacy*, we are told:

> For as long as there have been families, women have been
> experts in the realm of the emotions. Women understood
> their children's needs before their infants could speak; women
> soothed men's nerves; women comforted, cajoled, sym-
> pathized, loved. Yet a new generation of women have
> deliberately made themselves strangers to emotion. . . .
> Sometimes we went too far in controlling our emotions.
> Conflict had settled deep into our souls, making us unable
> to love even when we wanted to.[7]

Today I think I meet more and more women who have closed off their own "skin hunger" needs because it seems incompatible with the competitive world they have chosen to enter. In more than a few cases, they also struggle to meet the touching needs of their children. And children not adequately touched are often a tragedy in the making.

One can set moods anywhere, but home is the practice field. Someone has observed that whenever a follower of Christ walks into a room, everyone in the room benefits from the presence of God's Spirit if the believer is willing to let him work through his or her life. This is a marvelous challenge for someone like me. To think that I have the possibility of being the vehicle by which God will momentarily speak to others as I set moods is a great stimulation.

I have seen it happen. Some years ago, I was delighted with an incident on an airliner flying from Atlanta to Boston. It was during a strike of the air traffic controllers, so the anxiety of many of the passengers was plain to see.

The chief flight attendant must have sensed the unease of passengers because she set out to turn people's moods in another direction. As the plane took off, she informed us that the flight came to us "courtesy of Captain O'Brien. Let's give him a hand," she said. Strangely enough, the entire planeload of people broke into applause.

Later, this same flight attendant announced lunch. She and her team would be serving soup, she said, "and if you refuse my soup, I'll feel rejected." Again, levity and escape from anxiety.

Sometime afterward, she pointed out a landmark. "Those of you on the left can see New York City, and those of you on the right can see those on the left looking at New York City."

The entire spirit of that plane changed from nervousness to relaxation. We all wondered what this enthusiastic woman would say next. By the time we landed at Boston's Logan Airport, the passengers were applauding to thank her for having made our flight a rare experience.

Here was a woman who had taken nervous passengers

and redirected their emotional energy. She changed our mood; through humor we felt peaceful and supported. It's part of my purpose, too.

The path Gordon and I are following climbs steadily above Langwies. There is a place where one can look down into the valley. It gives a bird's eye view of the village, and we pick out the little church, the hotel, and the bakery. We can see people entering and leaving the store where Hans-rudi makes his bread and Norma sells it. It is more than a business they are running. They care for the people of their village and of the valley. You sense that driving purpose the moment you meet them.

Your care for others is the
measure of your greatness.
LUKE 9:48, TLB

CHAPTER THREE
The Kiss That Made Greatness

As our walk lenghtened, Langweis became a distant memory and our fatigue and hunger grew. It was important that we were sensitive to each other as well as to our own needs. The person with the stronger constitution yielded to the weaker. Conflicts were avoided, and the trip became enjoyable. Who knows, I think to myself, I might even be willing to do this again.

American artist Benjamin West used to tell friends that his career was launched on a day in his childhood when his busy mother asked him to take care of his younger sister, Sally. Hoping to please his mother, Benjamin determined to surprise her upon her return with a painting. Thus, he attempted a "portrait," he said, and the subject was sister Sally herself.

As one might imagine novice artists or small boys to be, West was far less than tidy about his effort, and soon paint seemed to be splattered everywhere. But when Mrs. West returned, she wisely ignored the mess that would normally have sent most mothers into a tailspin. Instead, she focused only on her son's performance as an artist, exclaiming with enthusiasm as she looked over his shoulder, "Why Benjamin, it's Sally." And with those words she stooped down and kissed her delighted son on the cheek.

"That kiss," Benjamin later reflected, "made me a painter."

It's possible that Benjamin West's mother never remembered the occasion and would have been surprised if anyone had told her years later that such a simple, instinctive reaction as a kind word and a kiss for her son had empowered him to pursue the artistic life. How often does one make a substantial contribution in the life of another and never realize its significance? Answer: Often!

Among the good things the mother of Benjamin West practiced that day was sensitivity, a second quality I have included in my personal purpose statement. In her case, she did it by being in touch with the most important issue of the moment: Benjamin's need for approval. Ignoring her own inconvenience, she concentrated on what was important to her son's sensibilities. And in so doing, she poured strength, vision, and encouragement into him.

Some would not have seen what West's mother saw. They would not have gotten past the splattered paint on furniture and surfaces where it didn't belong. Still others, if they had taken in the painting of sister Sally, might have been tempted to comment on the crudity of the figure in terms of proportion or perspective.

But not this mother. Somehow she understood, consciously or unconsciously, how one treats a person who is trying to express himself. Is it too dramatic to suggest that she sensed that an artist might be in the making? Could that be why she chose to ignore the mess of the present and plug into the possibilities of tomorrow? Did she determine not to be preoccupied with a "painted" living room and envision instead a studio with an artist at work? Was all this behind a kiss and an approving word? We do not know the answer to those questions, but we do know that her son interpreted her action as an endorsement, and it started him on the track of a great American painter.

While reflecting upon that story, I have wondered how many would-be artists, writers, and musicians never received the start given to Benjamin West because, at a key, vulnerable moment, they were crushed rather than kissed by mothers, fathers, or "friends" who lacked the sensitivity to nurture a wonderful gift in the making. Similarly, how many men and women in this world have desperately needed a word of grace, a comforting gesture, or an affirming touch and failed to receive it because those around them were not sensitive enough to realize how important it might be in a moment of failure or impending crisis or greatness.

Go back with me to Mary and her worship of Jesus in the home of Simon the Leper. If Mary exerted a massive influence on the mood of the men in the room that night, it was because she exercised sensitivity. Apparently, she was the only one there who read the signals that the coming days were going to be different than anyone else anticipated. She was the only one who felt a foreboding, a sorrow, and a pressure within the heart of the Lord. No one else there picked up those signals. The disciples were busy feasting in a manner that would precede a week of religious celebration. The contrasts between the sensitivities of Mary and the others are important to note.

When Mary began to act on the basis of her insight, the other diners, in their ignorance, were irritated by her actions. One of them, Judas, was put off by Mary's use of expensive perfume. In his brusque manner, he compared her tender actions to something valuable being poured down a rathole. In a few words, he attempted to cheapen a noble intention.

"Leave her alone," Jesus rebuked him. "It was intended that she save this perfume for the day of my burial." In other words, Mary was right on target, and Jesus was doing for her what Benjamin West's mother did for him. What Judas tried to cheapen, Jesus gave even greater value. Sensitivity returned.

When I incorporated the word *sensitivity* into my personal purpose statement, it was because I had come to believe that this is one of the most important qualities any woman must have if hers is to be a life of Christ-like servanthood. Sensitivity—the ability to read the "signals"—causes us to understand where to best position our resources and capabilities for the building of other people. If one is not sensitive, then one does not usually have a clue as to how best to serve. Where there are insensitive people, there is an increase of hurt, squelch, and discouragement.

But the sensitivity of which I speak in my purpose involves more than just reading the "signals" of the events that are going on around us. Sensitivity also means reading the "signals" that are being sent from within. In other words, I wish to enhance my sensitivity to my external world and my internal world so that one is in touch with the other.

Earlier in my life, I think I tried so hard to be sensitive to people and events beyond myself that I may have failed to monitor appropriate messages within myself. Thus, trying to be helpful to others, there may have been times when I denied myself that which was necessary to my ongoing spiritual and emotional health.

Sensitivity, then, is the development of an ability to look beneath the surface of events and people and ask the questions: What do these things mean? What is needed? And what can I contribute?

Those were questions that I see Mary of Bethany dealing with as she bowed before Jesus. Why her tears? Sensitivity, I am suggesting, to the coming suffering of Christ and her desire to comfort him—and sensitivity to her own grief because she understands that she will soon experience a great loss, one too great to put into words.

When there is a lack of sensitivity, people can be deeply hurt. We see that sad fact all the time.

I have borrowed a term from Esther Howard who, years ago, wrote in *Faith at Work* magazine about what she called IALAC. I-A-L-A-C, meaning *I am lovable and capable*, is that sense of self-assurance necessary to the inner health of every one of us. When we know God personally, we draw this sense of belonging and competence most powerfully from him. In the more immediate sense, however, most of us receive it through other people, just as Benjamin West received a portion of it from his mother when she looked over his shoulder. But we only receive it when people are sensitive.

It is possible to build this IALAC into one another, and, sadly enough, it is possible for us to take it away from each other in our insensitive moments. In other words, this IALAC is generally increased or diminished according to the sensitivity of those about us who, reading our signals, contribute to our sense of value and usefulness just as we hope we will to them.

To illustrate more fully the concept of IALAC, Esther Howard described the rather sad fictional day of a boy she called Peter whose experience seems the opposite of Benjamin West's. Peter, she wrote, imagined that his own IALAC actually hung about his neck like a gigantic cookie. Depending upon the actions of others toward him, affirming his competence and value as a person, Peter's IALAC "cookie" either enlarged or crumbled.

For example, when Peter dressed for school early that day, the IALAC gleamed prominently on his chest, and he was delighted with the thought of proudly displaying it for anyone who was interested. But his reverie was harshly interrupted when he heard his mother angrily shout, "Peter, get yourself down here before I come after you!" With the cutting sound of that shrill voice, a small piece of the IALAC hanging about his neck fell off and disappeared.

When the boy arrived at the breakfast table, his father was already hidden behind the *Wall Street Journal*. There were no words exchanged between the two until Peter accidentally spilled his milk. Unfortunately, some of the milk splattered on his dad's suit, and so Peter heard his father's first words of the day to him: "You clumsy . . . ! Look what you've done!" A second time that morning, Peter felt his IALAC grow lighter and smaller as another piece of it dropped away. The words of his father, like those of his mother earlier, had the effect of an acetylene torch on his sense of well-being.

Continuing her tale, Esther Howard further described Peter leaving his half-eaten breakfast and heading for the spot down the street where he would meet his best friend for the walk to school. But the walk did not go well because his friend seemed to ignore him, and the IALAC around Peter's neck crumbled a bit more. Nothing was helped, of course, when he dropped his lunch sack and it split open, causing several kids who had joined the walk to laugh at his plight. Peter's IALAC took still another beating.

At school, his teacher scorned his sloppy writing, and at recess his playmates called him a sissy. The whole day seemed to go that way. The IALAC, once sizable and visible in the early morning hours, seemed on the verge of disappearance, and when he felt that happening, Peter began to compensate for its loss. He decided, for example, that when he got home he'd tell his mother he was sick. Maybe she'd offer medicine or something that would provide attention and reaffirm his value and his competence.

But when he got home, his mother wasn't there, and that meant there was no medicine, no "something." Instead, what was there was a note that read, "Take the TV dinner out of the freezer and turn the oven to 425 degrees. I'll be back at 5:30."

By now Peter had lost the will to go out and play or to do anything constructive. He simply slumped in a chair and watched television. At 5:30, his parents came home. The good news was that Peter had taken the dinners out of the freezer; the bad news was that he'd forgotten to turn on the oven. Both of his parents commented in his hearing that their son was irresponsible and could never seem to remember anything.

When dinner was finally served, Peter sensed a hope of something good about to happen when his dad asked him about school. But just as he started to answer, the telephone rang and his father left the table in the middle of his sentence. When he returned, there was something else on his mind. By now, it was hard for Peter to remember that his IALAC had ever existed.

Howard writes, "When Peter went to bed that night he lay thinking about the little piece of the 'I' that was all he had left. He felt so sad and lonely that he put the pillow over his head so that no one could see him suck his thumb. It was the baby thing to do, but the only way he knew to comfort himself for what had happened to his IALAC that day."

Esther Howard ended her description of Peter's sad but not untypical day by noting that the boy wished there were a way to explain his feelings to his parents so that tomorrow he wouldn't have to watch his IALAC being torn apart all over again. "But he fell asleep before he could think of anything."[1]

The tale of Peter's day reminds me that we are dealing all day long with people (young like Peter or old like his parents) who are living with similarly accumulated incidents and who, like Peter, come to feel and act as if they also are unlovable and incapable. This perception becomes hardened; it becomes a personal view of life, a version of one's own reality.

I could be a person like that had it not been for those who were sensitive enough to build my IALAC. Realizing that, I have come to see the importance of giving IALACs to others whenever I can. As with Mrs. West, we can make a positive difference, or, as in the fictional account of Peter, we can do just the opposite.

But I noted earlier that there is also a dimension of sensitivity that looks within, that begins with self-understanding: knowing who we are and what makes us act the way we do so we can then reach out with confidence to others in their worlds with what they need.

I remember having to face up to this a few years ago when I watched our daughter, Kris, begin planning for college. At the time, she was looking forward to rooming with a special friend. One evening I commented to her, "You two won't even be homesick when you get to college; you're so close in your relationship."

"Yeah," Kris responded, "you're right. We were saying that very thing the other day. No homesickness for us."

Ouch! Those seemingly innocent words cut deeply! But why did they hurt? Should I have forgotten the pain and pressed on with other things? Should I have simply told myself to grow up? Be spiritual? Stop being a possessive mother?

Frankly, it was a moment for me to be sensitive to myself, a moment for me to be in touch with my emotion, to discover a truth about myself. Hadn't I prayed regularly for my daughter to have such a friend? Yes, I had. Hadn't I known that eventually our second and last child would leave our nest? Of course. Then why was I consumed with such sadness when Kris told me point-blank that she and her friend would make it just fine without their homes, without their mothers?

I left the room where Kris had made her remark to get a grip on my feelings and thoughts. I had to name whatever it was that was simmering within. When I had done that, I went back to her. I decided it was time for an honest admission between us so that we could be even more genuine in the time to come.

To blend sensitivity to action, we must attempt to name

the feeling or inner circumstance, whether it is within us or in someone else, and having named it, engage in an appropriate action that causes growth, comfort, rebuke, and reconciliation. In this case, I had to be sensitive to the sadness that was going on in me and, at the same time, sensitive to the joy of opportunity that was bubbling inside of Kris. Those two moods, seemingly counter to one another, had to be named and reconciled.

Kris always studied in her bedroom at her bedside. She would kneel with her papers spread all over her bed. So in order to talk face to face with her, one had to "knee up" to the other side of the bed. And that's what I did.

"Kris, it seems important that I tell you what I'm feeling right now—not only for my sake, but also for the years ahead when you go through these same things as a mother. I want you to know me not as a plastic, unfeeling, have-it-all-together person, but as one who struggles day after day to understand what's going on inside of her."

Kris listened, and I went on.

"You know how I've been praying for a friend for you who would understand and appreciate all that you are. Half of me is grateful for the answer to that prayer. But the other half of me grieves because I am slowly losing you. I know that I'm not losing you in actuality; but it feels like that."

At that, my eyes began to leak, and instinctively Kristy reached out to me and said, "Oh, Mom, am I making it harder for you?"

"No, not at all," I responded. "This all needs to be. But I want you to know that I've never gone through releasing my last child before, and I may blow parts of the process. I hope you can help me by being patient and know that I'm trying to do it the best way I know how. Plus, I want you to know how proud I am that you can make friends and plan a new world in which you are going to be more and more of what God wants you to be."

We two women—the younger and the older, the mother and the daughter—embraced in one of the tenderest moments of sensitivity that love can bring.

There is great power in sensitivity when we lead with it. My imagination prompts me to wonder what sort of a dinner Jesus would have had if Mary had ignored her sensitivity to his emerging suffering. Would he have sat there, his loneliness and sense of isolation increasing, as everyone around him carried on as if nothing of significance were about to happen? Would not the night have been drenched in superficiality, the real issue of the cross ignored?

Then I think of Esther Howard's fictional account of Peter and realize, with sadness, that every day scores of people go off to school and work or stay at home and see their IALACs dwindle because no one is sensitive enough to build their sense of value and competence.

But there is also Mrs. West who accelerated her young son on his path to greatness with a kiss and a word. And I remind myself that sensitivity is such a simple thing. When used in concert with other gifts—among them, generosity and affection—it becomes a powerful element in the human kit of people-building tools.

And so sensitivity has become a part of my mission. Like Mary of Bethany, I will deliberately choose to look into the lives of people and, when necessary, into myself to find out what's really happening. Appropriate action flows from understanding.[2]

CHAPTER FOUR
A Gift Remembered Forever

When you're far from home and friends, unfamiliar with the language, and unsure of your destination, your choice of a walking partner is key. He or she needs to be not only a sensitive person but also willing to go to any limit to preserve your life and well-being. Knowing Gordon was such a person brought me much comfort as we cimbed upward.

We know only a few facts about Mary of Bethany. We know that she had a sister, Martha, and that it's likely they would have had occasional clashes of personality; Martha appears to have been a doer while Mary seems to have been a reflective kind of woman. Her contemplative nature probably prompted Mary to value every moment in the presence of Jesus, and that caused her to see little reason to be interested in anything else except to listen to what he might have to say. Because I am more like Martha by nature, I am drawn to what Mary's strengths offer to stretch my growth.

When I ponder what little we do know about Mary and

weigh the impact she has had upon me, I realize all over again how the totality of our lives can often be summed up in a very few things when life in this world is over. Usually those things are qualities of character rather than quantities of things, contributions rather than achievements.

How old was Mary when she died? We don't know. Did she have a career? We don't know. Was she well-known or popular? We don't know. Did she leave a large estate? We don't know. Was she physically attractive? We don't know that either. But we do know this: She was capable of setting moods, of discerning them in others, and of giving her very best when the occasion called for it.

Let me highlight the third of those three things that Mary did that night at a men's dinner. I call it *serving sacrificially.*

When the dinner held in Jesus' honor was concluded, John wrote that Mary knelt at the feet of Jesus and opened a container holding an expensive perfume from the Orient. As she poured it over his feet, the odor filled the room. Some, if not all, of those looking on were shocked. Unlike us, they grasped the magnitude of this act and found it hard to believe she would do it.

It is difficult for us to completely appreciate Mary's gesture some two thousand years and several cultures removed. But perhaps we can understand the significance of the moment if we realize that the expensive perfume represented her life savings, her insurance, her dowry. Once the container was opened, the contents were lost. The perfume could not be reclaimed, only offered for the purpose of the moment.

So what was Mary doing? She was giving a gift of supreme personal value as she expressed devotion to Christ. Mary was giving the best that she had, nothing withheld. What must this have meant to the Lord?

Isn't her action a mirror of what the Lord was about to do on the cross? Did it not symbolize, both in the spirit of giving and in the value of the perfume, a self-emptying gift? A total outpouring? At that moment of sacrificial giving, the focus

66

of the story is only upon two people—Mary and Jesus. Neither seems daunted by the negative opinions of others.

Mary had a right to keep this one thing for herself. What could it matter? And yet by giving it, Mary was outwardly expressing an inner affection that no one else in the room could appreciate. The Lord responded to her generosity with the only recorded affirmation of its kind in Scripture: "I tell you the truth, wherever the gospel is preached throughout the world, what she has done will also be told, in memory of her."[1] And so, even in this mention of her story, we fulfill his promise once more. But isn't it possible that Jesus also meant that Mary is remembered every time someone gives all they have—as she did?

The third leg of my purpose statement, the one that reflects Mary's sacrificial giving, is the toughest for me to implement. You could say that all of us have an alabaster box of some kind—certain things or areas of our lives we hold on to and with which we will part only in a moment of extraordinary importance. The spirit of the times in which we live says of those things: Cling to them; risk them only when you can increase their value.

Mary's gesture runs counter to this modern spirit. She challenges that part of my nature that wants to hold on tightly and take few risks. Few of us, if any, are automatically generous; we must learn it from Christ himself and reaffirm its importance often. Generosity requires purposeful activity because, unless I make it a specific intention, it will not happen.

Usually, about the time I think I may be making progress in this particular grace, I experience a day when I see how far I have to go in order to reach Mary's level. Francois Fenelon's words make me feel as if he were talking to me when, centuries ago, he wrote:

> *You were not yet as detached from earthly things as you flattered yourself you were. We never know ourselves until the time of trial comes, and God only sends such trial to*

undeceive us as to our superficial detachment. God allowed Peter's terrible fall in order to undeceive him as to the real nature of a certain outward fervor and very frail courage on which he was most vainly relying.[2]

Let me say it again: In my mission statement, I purposed to serve or give sacrificially because if I did not make generosity of soul a conscious objective, worth reviewing every day, I would become preoccupied with the opposite trait of accumulation or self-centeredness.

To me, sacrificial giving reaches its peak when it comes directly from a heart that is overflowing with gratitude for life and seeks to display that gratitude. This is a long way from "ought-to" giving ("it's my duty") which can so easily plague us and deny us the joy that Jesus taught was to be found in giving. The giving takes no inventory as to what has been given, and it does not make appreciation from others a condition for its gift.

I have a dear mother and father who have taught me this value through their own modeling. As they have moved into the senior years, they have chosen to slowly distribute their "stuff" rather than fall into the trap of accumulating more.

When our son-in-law Tom, an enthusiastic camera buff, had his camera bag with all of its contents stolen, it was instinctive for my dad to think about how he could respond to this need. So he gathered his camera, all of the lenses and gadgets he had accumulated, and a lovely case that protected it all and shipped them off to Tom. When Tom asked Dad why he was giving away such expensive equipment, Daddy said, "I'm not going to be around much longer. I'd like to get rid of things now and enjoy watching others use them." My mother and dad have given themselves and their "gifts" away ever since I can remember. The object of their desire is eternal, not temporal.

The inspiration of my dad's act of generosity and many

others like it has stuck with me through the years. What has God given me that I can give to others? Why hold on? Why try to impress others through a value system based upon things that are going to burn up or rot some day anyway?

But sacrificial loving comes not only in releasing things but in the giving of oneself. David Seamands once preached a sermon from the Older Testament story of Rebekah who became the wife of Abraham's son Isaac. Abraham had sent a servant to Nahor, his homeland, to find a wife for Isaac. How was he to make a selection? The servant prayed, asking God to cause the right woman to offer water from the well not only to him but to his camels also. This would be the sign.

And that is exactly what happened. A woman, Rebekah, when asked by the servant for a drink, responded affirmatively and added, "I will provide water for your camels also."

This was no small generosity Rebekah proposed. Seamands reminded his audience that camels have a large water capacity: When thirsty, they can drink about thirty gallons. And the servant's camels were thirsty. There were ten of them, and so, Seamands said, we were reading about a woman who was willing to draw approximately three hundred gallons of water for a stranger. That was what one might call second-mile giving—or should we call it "extra-gallon" giving? Whatever the name, it is sacrificial giving or serving.

Seamand's sermon has become an inspiration to me. When I am asked to do something in our home, something menial or inconvenient, I say to myself, "Gail, are you prepared to water their camels also?"

Most of us love to have our work recognized and appreciated. Rebekah's work was, but at first, Mary's was not. Instead, some belittled her gift. But Mary paid little or no attention. Her gift was for the Lord, and his affirmation was enough.

This business of sacrificial giving as a mission in life increases in significance to me each time I hear one more message from our culture saying there are other values that are more important. I am confronted with a daily choice: Will I give or take? As a follower of Christ, I desire to renounce the spirit in the air that says that rights, power, notoriety, and objects are the supreme values.

In his autobiography, Malcolm Muggeridge, while writing about various power-hungry leaders in the past few centuries, notes:

> *Jesus proclaims his Kingdom as the antithesis of power; as a kingdom of love. Pilate and Herod and the Sanhedrin all operated in terms of power; so, on an enormously greater scale, did Caesar; but Jesus himself disdained power, scorned it, found wisdom in babes and sucklings, and picked his disciples among fishermen. None the less, it is he, not the others, who are remembered,* whose birth, ministry, death, and resurrection have provided the greatest artists, writers, composers, architects, with their themes and their inspiration. *Without power, he was almighty; with power, the others, like fireflies, shone awhile and then disappeared* [emphasis mine].[3]

Muggeridge went on to point out that Jesus resisted Satan's temptations to use miracles in order to generate power. In fact, he renounced the satanic alternatives because they had to do with power. Instead, he embraced a life-style of love, fulfilling the destiny that was prepared for him—to die on a cross hearing shouts of ribaldry and abuse in order that a great new wave of redeeming love might come to this world.

Of what use is the threefold mission statement I have described? It serves, first of all, as a direction setter for each day. Each morning I reaffirm my commitment to these purposes and then think of them in terms of what I face for the day. I find there is great value in programming my mind to think of all of the day's events in terms of mood setting, sensitivity, and sacrificial loving. The exercise rebukes any energy of rebellion and selfishness that might be lurking in my dark side waiting to tempt me in other directions.

Who are the most specific targets of my mission? For me personally, the first person in my field of purpose is my husband. In days gone by, it included my children until they left the home in their adult years. I've never regretted the choice to make my husband the central object of my mission in life, and I'm even more thankful today about this choice than I was in previous years. It's held me through challenging times when I might have crumbled without it. Others in our generation and those past have encouraged me in this pursuit.

Beyond my husband and our family, my purpose extends to a host of special friends—those in our immediate Christian family and those in my world whom I have the privilege to know. And sometimes my purpose calls for moments of loving and giving to people I'll never know and who will never recognize or thank me.

At Christmastime, for example, Gordon and I have made a vow that any time we are out Christmas shopping, we will never pass a Salvation Army officer with a bell without slipping a dollar in the pail. A recent crosstown walk in New York City, where the Army seemed to have established a presence at every corner, grew rather expensive but very satisfying. I would never engage in a giving game like this except that it springs out of a sense of purpose.

Coretta Scott King once wrote to a friend and reflected upon the purposes in her life that found their realization in her generous support of her husband, Martin.

> *The amazing and wonderful and terrible things that came later in our lives created no problems between us. I had decided I would become the wife of Martin Luther King, Jr., and though I could not foresee what the future held—his leadership of the Civil Rights Movement, the work and the*

strain, the dangers, his fame, and the tragedy—there was never a moment that I wanted to be anything but the wife of Martin Luther King.[4]

In one of his speeches, Dr. King spoke of greatness, and I can't help but wonder if he didn't have Coretta in his mind when he said:

> *Everybody can be great. Because everybody can serve. You don't have to have a college degree to serve. You don't have to make your subject and your verb agree to serve. You don't have to know about Plato and Aristotle to serve. You don't have to know Einstein's theory of relativity to serve. You don't have to know the second theory of thermodynamics in physics to serve.* You only need a heart full of grace. A soul generated by love [emphasis mine].[5]

Has anyone ever heard the name of Biddy Chambers? Hardly anyone today. Millions of Christians know of her husband, Oswald. Yet what most do not know is that few of us would ever have heard of Oswald Chambers, much less profited from his ministry, had it not been for Biddy.

Recently, I read through Oswald's diaries, written during the final two years of his short life. I was surprised to learn that this noted author whose name appears on more than thirty books, most notably *My Utmost for His Highest*, "actually never set out to write a single manuscript!" Rather, his biographers tell us that except for his diaries none of his thoughts would be available today were it not for the meticulous care of Biddy. She served her husband well by taking shorthand notes of his talks and transcribing them for publishing long after his death. Only eternity will tell what this one woman's choice to serve has meant to millions since 1917.[6]

Biddy was apparently that kind of woman in much that she did. When the Chambers were making a decision as to whether or not God was calling them to go to Egypt where Oswald would be a spiritual director to World War I troops, he said of her: "Biddy is keen on the thing and will never do anything but back me up, no matter what it costs her."[7]

I am deeply moved by a private comment like that. It tells us Mrs. Chambers was prepared to pay a high cost so that many others could receive untold encouragement.

Another of my long-time encouragers, Maria Taylor, now dead for a hundred years, was way out ahead of me in the pursuit of her purpose. Maria was the wife of Hudson Taylor, the founder of the China Inland Mission. Of her, it was said by her biographer:

> *Hudson could lean hard on her, drawing vigor from her spiritual maturity, her tranquillity and faith, her unwavering affection. She gave him and their work all she had, every ounce of strength, every thought that crossed her intelligent mind, all the force of her love. She allowed him to drain her, and if sometimes his demands were unconsciously selfish, she was no more aware of it than he.*[8]

Mrs. King, Mrs. Chambers, Mrs. Taylor. All women spurred on by a purpose: to serve. In their cases, their husbands were the primary beneficiaries. In turn, all of us have been beneficiaries.

These, then, are the reasons for the way I have constructed my mission or purpose. It may not sound like one another woman might write, but it keeps me going on good days and hard days. For me, it makes a lot of sense. I look forward to telling Mary of Bethany someday how her choices challenged me in the formulation and living out of this statement:

> *I purpose, through the power of Christ within, to follow the example of Mary of Bethany who chose to set moods, be sensitive, and serve sacrificially. Fully aware that my own*

growth is in process, taking a lifetime, I will live patiently, relax, and enjoy the journey.

Fail-safe? Absolutely not! Constantly achievable? No way! Always carried out? You're kidding! But a direction in which to move each day? Absolutely.

Ella Tweeten was the mother of Margaret Jensen, author of a number of delightful books such as *First We Have Coffee*. Momma, as she was known, instinctively understood this business of setting moods, being sensitive, and serving sacrificially. Because I have experienced all of these graces through the lives of both Margaret and her daughter Jan Carlberg, I have carefully noted her life.

A few days before Ella died, Margaret Jensen recalls that Momma lay in bed reminiscing over her long life. She spoke of all the years she had given to the "making" of her husband and seven children, what it had meant to her, and what she perceived it had cost her. But she wanted her daughter Margaret to know that every moment had been worth it. No regrets.

"I realize now that all the while I was 'making' all of you, *Jesus was making me*," she told Margaret.

On the day Momma died, she gave Margaret her offering envelope for church. Being a person of routine, she had already stuffed it with her weekly gift, days before worship. Hers was a one-day-at-a-time climb through life. It was not focused on preoccupation with self, but a generosity that was independent of what those around her thought or how they lived. Her eyes were on the One who gives power to climb. If he cheered her on, what else mattered?

TWO

Carrying Little Weight

CHAPTER FIVE
Lightening the Load

The walk from Langwies to the top of the Strela Pass is beautiful, but it is no stroll through a park. The innkeeper estimates the walking time to the top at three hours. But it's probably more like four to the top and four back. That's eight hours on our feet. Add another two more for rests and quick detours to photograph a wildflower or see a special sight and eat a picnic lunch. The sum of it all is a long, long day.

It also means that you had better be careful about what you take along. When you fill the pack on your back early in the morning and you are high with enthusiasm, you've got to think about how you're going to feel at four in the afternoon when you are barely staggering back to Langwies. Are you sure you want to carry all that weight?

With these thoughts in mind, we fill the packs we'll carry on our backs but quickly realize they're too heavy to tote for eight hours. So we empty them again to rethink what we really need for the walk. Do we need two cameras and all those lenses? Must we take that extra pair of shoes? Is it wise to carry all that fruit? Will a sweater substitute for a jacket? What is essential for a walk to the Strela Pass anyway? It's decision time, and some things simply have to be discarded and the weight reduced to the lowest possible level.

"There's got to be a parable here," Gordon says. (The two of us often think in terms like that. It's the way of a preacher's home.) We both laugh.

"Of course there is."

"Good, let me have it," he challenges.

"Scripture says, 'Lay aside every weight' in order to run the race of faith. Well, we're laying aside every unnecessary weight in order to walk to the top of the pass. If you believe that spiritual life is important, you have to make it a point to ask often: What weight am I carrying today that I don't need to carry, that I shouldn't carry, and that I can't afford to carry?"

"That's pretty good," Gordon says. "Keep working on it."

Not long after, we put our lightened packs on our backs and leave the Alte Poste Hotel. As we start up the pathway, I continue to think about my comment to Gordon about unnecessary weights. I've got more than a parable percolating in my mind. The issue of weights in the inner life becomes more and more real to me as we fall into a mutual rhythm and pace of walk.

Weights—guilt, despair, bitterness, hardness against God, the need to prove oneself and win, jealousy, and envy. These and many more are the things one has to look for because they bog down life's climb and make what should have been a delightful ascent into a disaster.

None of these weights in the spiritual dimension seems heavier to me than the weight of anger and resentment. This "baggage" seems to accumulate as time passes if it isn't identified and discarded. And if it isn't, one has to expend increasing amounts of energy simply to carry it.

Who of us does not know someone who is carrying such weight? Who of us hasn't carried this kind of weight for a while ourselves? Consider one woman who is deeply hurt by the failure of another and chooses not to forgive. In so doing, she effectively nails herself to that event and time and makes her climb a difficult one. Another woman, however, knows a similar betrayal and chooses to manage the pain and hurt by giving mercy and forgiving grace. She not only steadily moves beyond the event to further growth but gains a bit more strength and resilience to become an even more forgiving person in the future. One act of forgiveness usually begets another.

Forgiveness—discarding the weight of anger and resentment—is of particular interest to me. I know what it's like to face the challenge of forgiveness, and I am in touch with a significant number of women who have faced it, too. All of this has taught me that being a forgiving person may be one of the most important matters a modern Christian woman can pursue.

As our Western world becomes more caught up in non-Christian life-styles, and as spiritual warfare becomes increasingly more vicious in the Christian community, most of us are going to face the issue of forgiveness over and over again. A new generation coming into adulthood is no doubt going to have to learn how to forgive a parental generation it feels was too busy to give proper affection and affirmation. Women and men are going to have to learn how to forgive spouses who have succumbed to terrible temptations. Sooner or later it is probable that each one of us is going to face a major forgiveness moment with someone we love, and if we are not prepared for it, the times will be tough.

Forgiveness is more often a life-style of grace than a one-time act. We have fooled ourselves if we think that the resolve to forgive someone who has hurt us can be wrapped up in an overnight decision. That's an unreal expectation and an inhuman pressure to put upon ourselves.

More than one woman has written to me to share a struggle with forgiveness. Their letters usually sound like this one:

No one has to tell me that forgiveness is Christ's way when you've been betrayed. But just when I think I've given the gift of forgiveness, a whole new set of doubts and angers reenters my mind. It is as if I have to start all over again. Sometimes I can go for several weeks with no problem. Then when I least expect it, all the feelings and memories of the past pain come flooding back and I'm at square one again. Am I the only one who feels this way?

Naturally, the matter of forgiveness becomes harder or easier depending on whether or not the offender has asked for forgiveness and has shown great sorrow and remorse over what has happened. If there is none, the forgiver may overcome a natural tendency toward vindictiveness, but feelings of betrayal and hurt may not be so easily healed.

On the other hand, if the offender has expressed great remorse, there is the possibility of a most tender moment in a relationship. What will the offended party do with the repentance? For repentance is a two-way street: The repenter owns up to his or her responsibility, and the forgiver determines what to do with the repentance.

I am convinced that we do not learn to forgive in the hour of crisis, we actually train for it. Is it strange to say that in our best moments we prepare for the potential worst ones? In this case, we study the meanings of forgiveness and how it is portrayed in Scripture. We watch and learn from others who are going through situations needing forgiveness. And we monitor our own spirits to observe our progress in times of small irritation or conflict. Are we instantly vindictive or easily drawn to give grace?

Do we hold grudges easily? Is it difficult to disengage from hard feelings toward another who has offended us? Are there those with whom it would be difficult to sit down and pray because we harbor hostilities toward them? Asking such questions is imperative if we are to guard our hearts closely. For, to repeat myself, few things are more crippling to the person who wants to climb spiritually than the inability to forgive quickly and thoroughly.

Is there a greater example of forgiveness in all of history than the moment in which Jesus hung, dying, on a cross and, looking on those who cursed him and were responsible for his ultimate humiliation, said, "Father, forgive them; they do not know what they're doing." It's prompt. It's thorough.

The ability to forgive does not come naturally to most of us. As I said, we might acquire it first by studying its theme in Scripture. I've been particularly challenged by St. Paul.

The apostle who authored a large part of the New Testament through his letters never seems to have forgotten that he was, before anything else, a forgiven man. This was the gift given to him—first, by God, and then, by the church—even though he had been responsible for the incarceration, murder, and scattering of many Christians. Looking backwards to those days, he writes of himself: "I was once a blasphemer and a persecutor and a violent man." And then he goes on to add: "I was shown mercy. . . . The grace of our Lord was poured out on me."[1]

Later, when it was Paul's turn to suffer in various towns and villages where hostile people turned on him, he must have frequently said to himself, "Now I experience what I once did to other followers of Christ. What if the Lord had poured upon me the vengeance I deserved rather than the grace and forgiveness I needed?" Now this man who had formerly been so hardened and vindictive became gracious and kind, refusing to fight back at those who attempted to make his life so miserable.

Paul's refusal to be mean to his enemies reminds me of a comment Amy Carmichael made about the father of a friend who had suffered terribly from injustice. The experience was enough to have turned many of us into bitter cynics. But this man was different. When his daughter was asked what the effect of his suffering had been on her father, she replied, "It has left him unable to think an unkind thought of anyone."[2] You get the feeling that Paul worked at being this sort of man.

What would have been the effect of suffering upon Paul if he hadn't developed the instinct of a forgiving spirit? What would have been the outcome of his climb if he had chosen to carry the accumulated weight of hatred for those who threw stones, arranged for his beatings, or tried to discredit him?

The tiny mountain town of Lystra is the first good example. There a murderous mob had stoned Paul, dragged him outside the city, and left him for dead (Acts 14:19). When he recovered, he went on. But he came back later, whereas most of us would have avoided that city like a plague. He came back because he held nothing against those who had thrown the stones. The result? He met a young man named Timothy who became like a son to him and who carried on his apostolic ministry long after the old apostle was gone. Timothy would never have become Paul's protégé if a hardened, bitter spirit had caused Paul to stay away from Lystra.

Paul also performed admirably a second time when he was pitched into a jail at Philippi (Acts 16:23). Stripped and beaten, he and his companion, Silas, were placed in an inner cell, their feet fastened in chains. It would appear that the jailer maximized their discomfort before he himself went to a comfortable bed. It could have been a time for Paul and Silas o decry the injustices of the people who had jailed them and to plot the sort of vengeance they were going to bring down upon the town's authorities when they got their day in court.

But that wasn't the way it was. The two men prayed and sang in worship until about midnight when there was an earthquake. The jailer awakened and quickly decided to take his own life because he assumed a vengeful Paul would, by that time, have escaped.

CARRYING LITTLE WEIGHT

But Paul's *inner conditioning* once again surfaced. Instinctively, his concern was for the jailer—this man who had slept through the apostle's misery, this man who had more than likely either enjoyed Paul's earlier beating or made it happen himself, this man who had offered no medical treatment or suitable comforts.

"Don't harm yourself!" Paul cried out. Are there many of us who would have shown that concern? Would it not have been easy to say, "Let the man do anything he wants to himself; he has it coming?" We may not seek to cause direct harm to another, but we might not mind if one who is our enemy harms himself. Isn't that what the expression "Let him hang himself" really means? Paul's spirit was such that he not only refused to harm the jailer directly but also prepared to intervene if the jailer sought to "hang himself."

I think that when the earthquake shook down the prison walls, I would have run. Not Paul! He could have. But he stayed because of a heart preconditioned to forgive. And the forgiveness was set in motion before it was asked for.

Forgiveness is so aligned with Christ's actions on the cross that to embrace the one as the point of personal reconciliation with God is to embrace the other as a way of life. As Gary Inrig has pointed out, "Forgiveness is the one thing the enemy cannot counterfeit." Satan never received forgiveness; he can only oppose it. And when it prevails, he is grandly defeated.

In the Philippian jail story, everybody won. The jailer and his household became believers. Paul and Silas had their wounds dressed and were fed and welcomed into the jailer's home as friends. Question: Would the letter Paul later wrote to the young church at Philippi mean what it does to us today if Paul had not been the gracious man he was that night?

But wait. Sandwiched between the story of Lystra and Philippi is a third incident, this time one about an unforgiving, seemingly implacable Paul. I wonder if Luke highlighted it there with a lesson for readers like me in mind.

John Mark was the point of contention between Paul and his onetime companion, Barnabas. Earlier, Mark had shown himself unable to endure the rigors of the first apostolic journey and had turned back toward home (Acts 13:13). Later, Barnabas was willing to overlook that failure and give Mark a second chance; Paul was not.

The two men disagreed so strongly about the matter of John Mark's future that they parted ways (Acts 15:37-40). Imagine what Paul must have felt like later when he realized what his impulsive temper and unwillingness to show grace to Mark had cost him. Now he was estranged from his dear friend Barnabas, who had been the only one willing to take great risks to bring Paul into the church in the earliest days of Paul's faith. When Paul had been given the chance to give much the same kind of grace to Mark, he had failed.

Later, Paul would change his mind about Mark and make note of him as a highly profitable partner in ministry (2 Tim. 4:11). The Bible gives no indication of a connection, but I have often wondered if Paul's eager, forgiving performance in Philippi is, in part, the result of his having processed the harsh, severe lesson of his failure with Mark and Barnabas.

Who taught Paul to travel with lightness of spirit in the face of the terrible opposition he faced both from non-Christians and, sometimes, from people who called themselves Christians? Where did his practice of forgiveness come from?

Did it start with what he saw in the life of Stephen on the day he gave consent to the man's death? What did it mean to Paul when he heard the dying Stephen pray a prayer similar to Christ's, "Lord, do not hold this sin against them?"[3] That brief prayer must have banged about in Paul's soul for a long time afterwards.

Paul may have learned from Stephen that what happens to us when people hurt us won't matter years from now *unless* we have chosen to carry the resentful memory of it like a dead weight through life. But a forgiving spirit sheds that weight and springs us free for the better moments of the climb.

Was Paul's education in the art of forgiving also a product of his experience in the city of Damascus soon after he had received the heavenly vision of Christ on the approach road? Blinded and weakened, he must have been overwhelmed when Ananias, a prophet who had every reason to fear and resent him because of his murderous reputation, entered the room in which Paul was staying, laid hands on him, and said, "Brother Saul."[4]

Think of it! Paul must have expected anger—or at least a lecture. But instead, with the laying on of hands came the affirmation that things done in the past would not deter him from receiving the grace of God. Paul was a *brother!* What Stephen had started, Ananias continued. And Barnabas later sealed.

Sometimes forgiveness is not ours to give but to ask. It seems that most of us struggle on one side or the other of this issue. Either we have a hard time giving forgiveness or we have a rough time acknowledging that we need it. Both slow down the climb just as effectively. The inability to come to points of brokenness and acknowledge our own sin against God and others is a weight accumulator.

Recently, Gordon and I were told the story of a Christian layman who lives in the Midwest. One morning he was driving to the business he owned when it occurred to him to stop at a doughnut store and pick up some refreshments for his employees.

Caught up with his impulse, he quickly swerved from the fast lane of the freeway toward an exit where he knew he could find what he was looking for. In so doing, he failed to see a car in another lane and nearly caused a serious accident.

As he drove off the interstate, he noticed that the car he had cut off was following him. In fact, it continued to follow him right into the parking lot of the doughnut shop. When both cars were parked, the other driver got out of his car and stared in hot anger at the one who had come close to causing him an accident. Finally, the offended driver returned to his car and, in a show of disgust, left the parking lot.

As the car drove off, a frightened but very chastened man got out of his own car and took note of the license number. Upon reaching his own office, he made a phone call to a friend in the police department who provided him with the name and address connected with the license plate.

A few hours later, this man entered the office of the man whose car he had almost wrecked. As we heard the story, he said, "I'm the man who cut you off on the freeway. I've come to tell you that I'm very sorry."

The second man must have been speechless. But when he recovered from his surprise, he invited his visitor to sit down. The ensuing conversation became friendly. Before their visit ended, the man asking forgiveness was able to introduce the other man to the issue of faith in Jesus Christ. I believe this never would have happened if the man had not taken the asking of forgiveness seriously.

The issue of forgiveness changed for me the day I began to look at the one to be forgiven from a different perspective. A young Christian student leader helped me with this.

"There is a large difference between captives and enemies," he said. "When we encounter someone who has offended us greatly in one way or another, we need to see him as a spiritual captive, not an enemy." He repeated himself for emphasis. "No matter how distasteful one's actions may seem to be, you must visualize him as a captive and not your enemy."

Later, I looked up the exact meaning of captive in a dictionary. "A prisoner," is one definition. "One who is enslaved by a strong emotion or passion." I saw the perspective this young man wanted me to see.

The enemy of God's people loves to take people's wills,

passions, and actions captive. *Captives cannot free themselves.* They need someone to see them as captives who need releasing rather than as enemies to reject. It looks to me as if every place Jesus went he looked at people through this lens. Somehow, those broken enough to be in touch with their own condition saw hope and grace in the eyes of Jesus and were drawn toward him. Christ's hope? "That they will come to their senses and escape from the trap of the devil, who has taken them *captive to do his will*" (emphasis mine).[5]

I don't think Paul ever forgot what it felt like to be a captive. He speaks from firsthand knowledge when he writes to the Roman believers, "When we were utterly helpless with no way of escape, Christ came at just the right time and died for us sinners who had no use for him."[6]

In a more modern era, Corrie ten Boom has taught us this same lesson. For years she traveled the world, calling people to a forgiving spirit. This was no simple theological proposition she raised. Rather, it arose out of her own struggles in a German concentration camp in World War II. There she learned to see her enemies as captives, and her own spiritual "weightless" condition began.

In her book *Jesus, Man of Prayer*, Margaret Magdalen reflects much the same thing:

> *[When] the supernatural will to love has become entirely dominant over the natural will to take revenge, the pain is absorbed—redeemed—in the hurt person, and healing flows from that person to the original offender. A pain has been transformed by grace into a source of love for both people.*[7]

This was the weightlessness that an entire Christian community in California saw not long ago. On June 30, 1985, a deranged gunman entered a Chinese church, shooting and killing an outstanding Christian lay leader, Fook Kong Lee, and one of Lee's associates, before being fatally wounded himself. We had met Mr. Lee several months earlier and had been drawn to his sparkling humor and devotion to Christ.

When the *Los Angeles Times* covered the story, they noted the attitude of Fook Kong Lee's wife, Irene. She believed, she said, that her husband would have been happy that he had died in the pulpit serving the Lord. She went on to say that it was important to her that the ex-wife of the man who had killed her husband know that "I hold no bitterness against her for the shooting." Ironically, as the shooting occurred, the man's former wife was dropping their children off at Sunday school.

Perhaps the thing that challenged me most about Irene Lee's response was that she was speaking out of spiritual instinct. She did not have to work through a process of hate, anger, and acceptance. Forgiveness had long been a way of life before this tragedy, and it would be the same in the darkest moments of life.

Irene Lee's climb was a difficult one. But it was clear that day when she spoke to the *Times* that she was carrying no weight that would slow her up.

We talk glibly about forgiving
when we have never been injured;
when we are injured, we know
that it is not possible, apart from
God's grace, for one human being
to forgive another.

OSWALD CHAMBERS

CHAPTER SIX
Lightening the Load, Part 2

As Gordon and I take measured, brisk steps in the cool Swiss morning, I continue to ponder this issue of lightened loads, particularly what it means to renounce resentment and bitterness and pursue the giving of forgiveness. It's an important set of thoughts for me. As I said before, like many, I've had to face the challenge of forgiveness. And I know what it's like to be a free person when the choice to forgive is made. Fortunately, there are many whose lives challenge me to maintain this high road.

Like Corrie ten Boom, Viktor Frankl struggled to reflect a spirit of forgiveness in a German concentration camp during World War II. There he was stripped of everything except his wedding band. Later he wrote, "Everything can be taken away from a man but one thing: the last of human freedoms—to choose one's attitude in any given set of circumstances. . . ." Frankl was freer than his captors.

There are also contrasts to the spirit of Corrie ten Boom and Viktor Frankl. Dr. Armond Nicholi, well-known psychiatrist from Harvard University, has pointed out that both Karl Marx and Sigmund Freud had serious lifelong conflicts with their fathers. Neither man ever forgave his father for what he perceived were family injustices and oppressions. Their poisoned spirits seemed to mark their view of all human relationships. Both Marx and Freud died, Nicholi wrote, "bitter and disillusioned men, with little compassion for the common man."[1]

It seems to be a rule that when people choose to carry the weight of anger and resentment rather than a forgiving spirit, they run a serious risk. Paul put it this way when he admonished the Corinthians to forgive a man guilty of sexual sin who had openly repented:

> *A further reason for forgiveness is to keep from being outsmarted by Satan; for we know what he is trying to do.*[2]

Apparently, if Satan can keep someone from forgiving, and if he can keep them in bondage to resentments past and present, then he may well be able to direct the end of one's life toward the same bitter, disillusioned end Nicholi describes of Freud and Marx. The unforgiving person creates an environment within for the growth of other dangerous and ungodly attitudes.

A few months prior to a point in my life when I was going to need to forgive freely and instinctively one I dearly love, I had felt the promptings of the Holy Spirit to study Scriptures having to do with mercy and forgiveness. Looking back on those impulses and my response to them, I have been greatly comforted to realize that our Lord goes before us and means for us to be prepared rather than to crumble or become hateful when crisis comes. It suggests to me that if we are listening

CARRYING LITTLE WEIGHT

to his inner guidance and obeying it, we will have the assurance that we are in a state of preparation for what lies ahead. God does not allow the listening believer to fall into situations for which he or she will be unprepared.

In looking back on my own preparation, I see that forgiveness has always been an important value in our twenty-six years of marriage and family. In the first months of our relationship, Gordon and I determined that we would take seriously Paul's instruction not to end a day in anger. Upon that simple principle, I was able to build other principles of forgiveness.

For example, I became impressed with an insight once offered by David Seamands that the forgiver doesn't necessarily wait to forgive until he no longer hurts about what has been done to him. In fact, the quality of forgiveness might be called into question if one does not consciously face up to the genuine pain that an offense has caused him. Furthermore, when one forgives, Seamands observed, he is not whitewashing the seriousness of what has happened. He is not turning away from the fact that, on the human and divine levels, a law or a principle has been broken and it has to be made right. But he chooses to withhold judgment.

Another Christian thinker, David DuPlessis, taught me that when I forgive someone, I release him to become what God intends him to be. But if I refuse to forgive, I bind him to the moment and act of offense.

What DuPlessis suggests is precisely what happened when Paul heard Stephen forgive him. An earthly and heavenly "loosing"[3] was taking place because of one man's willingness to live forgiveness.

In the early days of our marriage, Gordon taught me something of the mechanics of forgiveness by simply being a forgiving person himself. He showed me how to be comfortable with admitting fault and asking for forgiveness by modeling it. For years, the children and I received his mercy and forgiveness when we erred. When a time came that he needed the same from me, there was no question as to how I would respond.

Today, I am most grateful for that *inner* conditioning that has made forgiveness a part of what I am as a person on a day-to-day basis. I need to be perfectly clear about what I am saying. In no way am I setting myself up as a model "forgiver." I'm not. But I will be bold enough to say that I do believe that the supernatural power to forgive can cooperate with our inner conditioning to forgive so as to make the process easier.

What saddens me is the person I meet who has never thought these matters through and then is ambushed by a terrible moment in which grace is desperately needed but he is unable to give it. Again, forgiveness is something you train for in the easy times and in the small things so that you can perform graciously in the difficult times.

But there is more to be said about forgiveness. I have also learned that when one needs to forgive, there is an important process to go through for total healing. The process takes time, and it is not without its moments of severe test. Sometimes I become irritable with those who try to teach us that these attitudes and actions can be developed and implemented overnight, never to be challenged from within. Let the forgiver beware: Forgiving is hard work, a supernatural work, and often emotionally tiring. On some occasions, one will feel as if they have to begin all over again as though back at square one.

Obviously, the severity and consequences of the hurt will influence the time it takes to work the process to completion. But there are, nevertheless, steps through which the giver of forgiving grace must pass. Let me lay them out in quick, identifiable concepts that have helped me a great deal.

1. RECOGNITION

Before we can begin the process of healing forgiveness, we have to *recognize* our hurt and name it for what it is. Someone has said that demons love to go unnamed. And someone else has said that you can't change what you cannot name. Maybe that's why Jesus always seems to have named or identified demons, sins, and inner attitudes that others would have liked to keep secret.

It's easy to deceive ourselves and pretend we aren't angry or to think that if we let things be, adverse feelings will go away. They won't. For a while we may be able to outrun negative feelings, but they won't stay away forever. They come back. Some things, like the spiritual cancers of resentment, hostility, and vindictiveness, require treatment. Massive treatment! But before anything can be treated, it has to be brought to the physician who specializes in that field and be diagnosed or named.

As I've already said, freeing captives is Christ's specialty. And when he enters the mix, he seems to look both ways: at the potential forgiver and at the one in need of forgiveness. *Both* the one who needs forgiveness and the one who can't forgive are captive!

A woman I know is typical of many with whom I have visited or corresponded. Her father sexually abused her for several years when she was a girl. It was only later in young adulthood that she found the memory of those awful experiences too painful to deal with. My friend had successfully jammed all of her feelings and angers down deep into her soul, and for a long time she assumed that what had happened could simply be forgotten like a bad dream.

But later that became impossible—especially when she married and began to face difficulties in sexual intimacy with her husband. It was not hard to find a connection between the struggles she was having in adult intimacy and the pain of her past, and she was forced to deal with the betrayal and abuse that had occurred in her childhood. Actions had to be named; feelings had to be identified; consequences had to be faced. Committing herself to the care of a competent counselor, my friend found healing for her wounds. But in the process, she discovered just how long a terrible, unresolved experience can lodge within a person if it is not named and dealt with.

This is a nearly universal reality for people who have experienced a deep personal hurt at the hands of another—a parent, a spouse, a friend, or a working associate. Until the issue is fully defined, its effects will probably not be brought under control.

When I converse with people like the woman I just mentioned, I challenge them with questions: Exactly what are we talking about? What feelings have been churning deep within you? When are you most likely to feel anger about this? What inhibitions has it brought to your life? Are there certain types of people who naturally raise hostility in you, and what does that mean? These are *naming* questions, and they lead a hurting person to a point of recognition as to what is really deep within. Of course, there are many, many similar questions.

2. RESOLVE

After recognizing the pain and its patterns, a person's second step in a forgiving experience is to deliberately *resolve* to forgive. This is where inner conditioning to be a forgiving person is so important.

CARRYING LITTLE WEIGHT

However, if the damage has been great, the resolve to forgive is still *only the beginning*. For forgiveness is a process that may have to go on for a long, long time until every ounce of anger or resentment has been identified and washed. We are far more complex than we may ever realize. About the time we think all of the residual memories and anger are gone, they raise their ugly heads again. Our *will to forgive* must take precedence over our feelings; we choose to forgive no matter what. In part, we make that choice because Christ forgave us and has called upon us also to forgive.

If we err in our resolve, we are in jeopardy of nailing ourselves to this point in our personal histories. Our bodies move on, but our spirits wither and harden.

Gordon and I have met persons for whom the past with its hurts and injustices is as real today as it was twenty years ago when the original transgression occurred: A businessman angry at a former partner whom he feels cheated him; a spouse who has never forgiven the other partner in a sad divorce; a young person who bitterly resents a father too busy to pay attention to him in his childhood.

These people and many like them leave a significant chunk of their lives behind them, fastened to the unresolved event. They are rarely free to fully love in the present or to look forward to the future with hope; something within them keeps them looking backward at events that were long ago buried in history but are as fresh in the unforgiving mind as if they happened only yesterday. This is captivity. This is bondage.

The resolve to forgive out of obedience to God is an unavoidable starting point. Perhaps that is what Jesus was accomplishing on the cross in the midst of his suffering— resolving to forgive his betrayers and captors, no matter what. These were the resolution moments; the process of forgiving grace would continue out of his heart forevermore.

3. RENUNCIATION

Judgmentalism and the desire for some form of vengeance are part of the angry and resentful heart. Let's be frank. The person who has been deeply hurt may wish to hurt back. To be greatly offended is to feel rejected, to feel devalued, to feel humiliated—in some cases, betrayed.

The normal human reaction to such feelings is to make the offender experience the same feelings so he knows what we have gone through. This may result in efforts to punish and inflict equal amounts of pain. The innermost parts of our lives can be very dark and mysterious places. Out of them come all sorts of impulses to hurt one another, and the instinct to return cruelty for cruelty dwells deep within us.

But forgiveness is the act of renouncing this desire. By renouncing, we choose not to be the agent of another's punishment or the carrier of vengeance. On paper this looks and sounds easy. It isn't! To renounce this right or instinct is a spiritual work, requiring determination and often—at least for a while—an hour by hour choice. At times the only motivation that helps is to see Christ on the cross making the same choice. "Father, forgive them, for they do not know what they are doing."[4] I see no desire at all on the part of Jesus to fight against those beneath him who are swinging the hammer or directing the operation. This is a stunning lesson.

Not all of us are tempted to display overt vindictiveness. Ours may be a more covert style. A few of us may take pride in the fact that we are not directly striking back at someone who has hurt us. But at the same time, we find ourselves delighting in circumstances where the person we'd love to harm looks bad before others. Or we can manufacture clever words and observations that put the squeeze on. Sometimes, acting as the wounded or innocent person, we can find insidious ways to permit or even encourage comments that cause the other to be further humiliated or disadvantaged. All the time we are satisfying ourselves that we are not deliberately causing these things. But a brutal honesty might force us to admit that we are indeed driven by the desire to punish.

The principle of *renunciation* suggests that the alternative to being vengeful people is actually to become protective people on behalf of the those who have offended us. I doubt that anyone outside of Christianity would ever propose such a thing. A revolutionary perspective like this one may demand a daily, if not sometimes hourly, affirmation because it is so unique and because it militates against the "get-back" attitude deep within.

I cannot forget Jesus' caring gestures toward Simon Peter on the night of the Crucifixion. Knowing of his imminent betrayal, Jesus warned Peter and prayed for him. Later in the garden, when Peter failed to join him in prayer, Jesus let him be and then offered him a spot by his side when it came time to face the temple guard.

Then there's the moment when Jesus sends word to his disciples that he's alive and sees to it, as one gospel writer says, that Peter gets a personal message about it all. Finally, there is that wonderful meeting on the Galilee shore in which Jesus makes it clear to Peter that the shameful events of previous days are not to be remembered, that the commission given earlier is still in force, that things between them are normalized.

At no point during all of this do we hear or see Jesus making Peter squirm or face public humiliation. Peter suffered enough from the consequences of acts for which he was responsible. There was no way Jesus was going to bring further punishment upon him.

I suppose what I'm seeing in all of this leads me to conclude that I need to be very careful that I do not take upon myself the role of judge and executioner when someone has sinned against God or against me. Who of us wouldn't like to do that at times; but who of us can afford to?

4. COVERING

From the life of King David comes a fourth mark in the forgiveness process. David was a man who seems to have understood that forgiveness means *covering* another's sin. That's another dramatic leap beyond renunciation.

Saul's pursuit of the young David through the wilderness must have exhausted the bodies and spirits of both men. At times Saul had invited David into his fellowship only to suddenly throw spears at him in an attempt to kill him. The king's mood vacillations were beyond belief. As others have observed, David's performance in the harsh moments was remarkable. Instead of throwing spears back at the king, David chose to duck and exit from his presence. We read of no vengeful words from the mouth of David at these times; only words of respect and sadness. It is clear that David was not going to be the source of trouble for Saul either by his mouth or by his actions.

Even when David had a perfect chance to end the conflict between them by killing Saul, he restrained himself. He would not make this man look bad. Then came the moment of Saul's disgraceful death. David could have seized the moment to exult in the king's demise as a vindication of his own position. He would have been justified in publicizing every single injustice, every betrayal, every sinister deed Saul had ever done.

But he didn't. Look at David's words as he mourns the death of Saul:

O Israel, your pride and joy lies dead upon the hills; mighty heroes have fallen. Don't tell the Philistines, lest they rejoice. Hide it from the cities of Gath and Ashkelon, lest the heathen nations laugh in triumph. . . . Both Saul and Jonathan slew their strongest foes, and did not return from battle empty-handed. How much they were loved, how wonderful they were—both Saul and Jonathan![5]

We've all seen ourselves as well as a score of other people use a similar moment wrongfully. It can be done quite skillfully. As a prayer request, as a testimony, as an item of "sharing" at a fellowship group. Everyone listens, and few stop to realize that what sounds like a justifiable piece of information is really someone's way of venting anger and vindictiveness.

D. E. Hoste, director of the China Inland Mission, said, "Looking back over these fifty years, I really think that if I were asked to mention one thing which has done more harm and occasioned more sorrow and division in God's work than anything else, I should say tale-bearing."[6]

David chose the high road in his painful relationship with Saul. What others would have exposed, he covered.

Now I think I understand where David's son Solomon picked up his admonition "love covers over all wrongs."[7] Had David's performance of forgiveness been a lesson for Solomon? And is there any connection between David's merciful spirit toward Saul and the fact that the New Testament contains no reference to David's great moral failure? Could this be the reason the only statement you will find there is that David was a man after God's own heart (Acts 13:22)? Did the Holy Spirit who oversaw the writing of Scripture make sure that David was covered at his most shameful moment when it came to referring to him centuries later? Is there a lesson for us here?

As James, the brother of the Lord, put it, "Watch what you do and what you think; for there will be no mercy to those who have shown no mercy. But if you have been merciful, then God's mercy toward you will win out over his judgment against you."[8] Love and forgiveness do indeed cover.

> *Love grows stronger when assailed;*
> *Love conquers where all else has failed;*
> *Love ever blesses those who curse;*
> *Love gives the better for the worse.*
> *Love unbinds others by its bonds;*
> *Love pours forgiveness from its wounds.*
> —Author Unknown

5. REBUILDING

The fifth step in the process of shedding the needless weight of resentment and anger is *rebuilding*. Frankly, this means that whenever possible the forgiver invests strong energies in not only covering the wrong but giving himself in loving ways to help the offender rebuild his or her life. When there is deep remorse for wrongdoing, a person will live with the sorrow of it forever, a spiritual limp, if you please. Our job as people of the cross is to *help lessen the limp*.

I love the story of Joseph of Egypt for many reasons. Suffering multiple adversities because of what his brothers had done to him, Joseph must have gone through enormous temptations to feel bitter and vengeful toward them. I've often wondered if he did not while away many idle hours pondering what he would say and do if he ever had a chance to meet up with them again. It has caused me to wonder if God did not have to let Joseph spend twelve or more years in slavery and in prison in order to grind such potential bitterness out of him. Were these years in which Joseph was learning not only the instincts of a leader but also the instincts of a forgiver? All I know is that when he left that dungeon to become one of the most powerful men in the world, he was a free man, unencumbered by pettiness, anger, or vindictiveness.

A careful reading of the biography of Joseph in the book of Genesis suggests that the brothers, on the other hand, lived in spiritual bondage and guilt over their hateful act of selling Joseph into slavery. Their guilt surfaced immediately when they came to Egypt to purchase food during a famine and appeared before Joseph, unaware that he was their long-rejected brother.

When Joseph and his brothers finally visited together, Joseph had both the power and the motive to be hateful and vindictive. He was in a position legally and had the right, according to the world's view of things, to hurt the brothers badly in return for what they'd done to him.

But he didn't. Later, in an emotional meeting, Joseph disclosed his identity to them, acknowledged his long-worked-through forgiveness toward them, and even made note that God had taken their evil act and squeezed good out of it. And then he went the extra mile by cautioning them from fear, saying, "I myself will take care of you and your families."[9] This is rebuilding love.

All the principles I've noted in preceding pages seemed to play themselves out in Joseph's life: *recognition, resolve, renunciation, covering, rebuilding.* They were all there in one way or another.

For me these have been the keys to the pursuit of being a forgiving person, one who refuses to carry extra weight on the climb. I know it to be a supernatural work of the Holy Spirit. Nothing less will do.

Years ago the *Reader's Digest* told the story of Edith Taylor who lived in Waltham, Massachusetts.[10] While Mrs. Taylor's story seemed then and now so extraordinary, it has challenged me because her graciousness in a terrible moment far surpasses my feeble abilities to forgive.

Mrs. Taylor's husband had held a construction job that took him overseas to Okinawa after World War II. The two agreed that a separation for a period of time was worthwhile for economic reasons. So Edith Taylor's husband crossed the Pacific while she stayed home.

Months of separation passed, marked by almost daily letters. But as time went on, the letters from Okinawa came less and less frequently. Then one day a letter arrived that changed Edith Taylor's life. Her husband wanted a divorce, he wrote. He'd met an Asian women whom he wished to marry. He wished a release from his marriage to Edith.

Sadly Edith agreed to the divorce but asked her husband to get in touch with her occasionally so that she would know something of the direction of his new life. He promised he would.

Some years passed. Edith's former husband fathered two daughters with his Japanese wife. As the announcement of each of these came, Edith would send a greeting and a gift.

Then one day another sad letter arrived. Mr. Taylor was terminally ill. Instinctively, Edith wrote to him to assure him that after his death she would do anything necessary to look after the welfare of his Asian family. And a day came when that became necessary.

After his death, Edith invited the daughters to come to America to live with her since their mother did not seem to be able to financially care for them. But when the daughters came, it soon became clear that the separation of mother and daughters was unbearable. So Edith made it possible for the mother to join them. In the years that followed, both women and the two daughters shared a Waltham, Massachusetts, home.

It was a remarkable act of forgiveness and rebuilding. When it was read by millions of Americans, not a few gasped, recognizing that they probably could not live up to such a standard. Perhaps that's why the article was entitled, *Could You Have Loved As Much?*

We continue our trek up the winding wanderweg toward the Strela Pass. On our backs are packs with the simple necessities for the coming hours: some chocolate bars, a bottle of water, a sweater, rain gear, and *one* camera. These are light packs. We've seen to that.

And the parable that has formed in my mind and heart means more to me than ever. The climb through life is a long and challenging one. No use making it any harder carrying the extra weight that can be discarded by grace, mercy, and forgiveness.

THREE

Keeping Healthy and Observant

Most middle-class Americans tend to worship their work, to work at their play, and to play at their worship. As a result, their meanings and values are distorted. Their relationships disintegrate faster than they can keep them in repair, and their life-styles resemble a cast of characters in search of a plot.
GORDON DAHL

CHAPTER SEVEN
The Sharpened Blade

"Look up there," my husband said to me as we pressed on toward the Strela Pass. I glanced in the direction he pointed. There, several hundred yards up the mountainside, I saw a man and a woman, probably husband and wife, cutting mountain grasses. The woman wore a full-length peasant dress, which surprised me. But it obviously wasn't awkward for her. The couple stood a few feet apart on a slope that seemed so steep that if either of them lost their footing, they would most likely tumble a long way before their fall could be checked by level terrain.

Both swung large scythes from side to side with the seeming effortless grace of ballet dancers. Their blades moved back and forth in half circles as though in concert with one another. We stood and watched for several minutes as they gradually moved through the grass, leveling it so it could dry in the sun and later be raked into piles and hauled away for winter feed.

Just as we were about to continue our walk, the two grass cutters stopped. As if a command had been given from somewhere, they both reached into their pockets and pulled out what appeared to be sharpening stones. Soon they were sweeping the stones back and forth along the curved blades of their scythes with the obvious intention of restoring the razorlike sharpness that is gradually lost as the scythe cuts through heavy grasses.

As with the cutting, the sharpening movements were balletlike, the motions of the man and woman each a reflection of the other. I was enchanted by this bit of artistic expression in the working lives of this Swiss farmer and his wife. Were they aware of the beauty in their physical actions? I asked myself. Was this a performance? Or merely a habitual rhythm to their work? Whatever the answer, it had to be only for their own good (or entertainment), for there was no audience that day except us, and there was no way they could have known of our interest in them.

But in that moment something else caught my imagination. As I stood pondering the couple's use of precious working time to apply the whetstone to their blades, I realized this pause in the grass cutting was not an interruption of their work; it was a part of their work—an effort to make the cutting easier and more effective. Theirs was a rhythm that made sense: The sharpening was followed by cutting, and more sharpening was followed by more cutting—in that order (the sharpening *first*) and appropriate proportion.

The person who wishes to keep climbing to the top in the spiritual journey might take the lesson of this farmer and his wife to heart. For just as their cutting would lose its effectiveness if there were no sharpening, the development of our inner spirits will regress when we deny ourselves occasions of what I am going to call the "sharpenings" of the interior life.

Let me state at the outset that the natural part of me resists the principle of sharpening. It seems more logical to the immature mind to spend one's time cutting rather than sharpening. That's the same part of the mind, by the way, that is more likely to long for motion, noise, and the company of people than such spirit-growing measures as Sabbath, silence, and solitude.

What do we mean by sharpening when we talk of it in spiritual terms? We're thinking of those exercises of the spirit that bring *renewal* to the relationship between a person and the Lord. Exercises that aid us in maintaining *mastery* over those things in life that seem to constantly try to master us. Exercises that make us more *effective* in living out whatever we have perceived to be our mission in the world.

But, as I wish to keep on noting, we often resist the sharpening exercises. Why? Why do many of us struggle, preferring the "cutting" motion and avoiding the "sharpening" motion?

Anyone who is interested in this subject can look at the lives of the church fathers and mothers. I think of such pioneers as John Wesley;, Thomas à Kempis, Brother Lawrence, or St. Teresa of Aolia, Amy Carmichael, and Susanna Wesley. . . . I realize that what made them so effective was their appreciation of this cutting/sharpening rhythm. In fact, the cutting and sharpening in their lives seem to have been so intertwined that it is often difficult to determine when one ended and the other began. They knew how to pause in the midst of the treacherous marketplace for just a few seconds and engage in the sharpening discipline. They also knew how to withdraw for hours, days, or even weeks to pursue it.

If you study them, the message becomes clear: No one can hope to persevere on the spiritual journey if the sharpening of the spirit is not a part of the cutting rhythm.

God has been calling people to various forms of sharpening since the beginning of time. What he calls us to is sometimes difficult and costly. It will involve renouncing things we would like to hold on to and embracing some things we would like to avoid. Sharpening is not glamorous; it is not easy; it cannot be reduced to "sugarcoated" methods.

The discipline of *giving a tithe* (10 percent) of our income, for example, is a form of sharpening. Tithing is a way of reminding us that our money and our possessions are not ours but God's. Tithing is a warning of sorts, a hedge against the human tendency to become materialistic with all the resulting problems of snobbery, recurring dissatisfaction, selfishness, and pseudo-independence.

Moses taught this form of sharpening to the chosen people before he led them toward the Promised Land where he knew they would become relatively affluent because of the great wealth in that land.

> *When you have eaten your fill, bless the Lord your God for the good land he has given you. But that is the time to be careful! Beware that in your plenty you don't forget the Lord your God and begin to disobey him. For when you have become full and prosperous and have built fine homes to live in . . . that is the time to watch out that you don't become proud, and forget the Lord your God. . . . Always remember that it is the Lord your God who gives you power to become rich.[1]*

The person who practices the sharpening discipline of tithing that Moses taught (see Lev. 27:30) will probably keep his financial house in order and will not succumb to the gross problem of overspending that is putting so many people into bondage today.

Many people are uncomfortable with tithing. They resist any standard that seems to tell them what to do with their money. They fear that if they were to give as much as a tenth of their money to the Lord, they would diminish their purchasing and saving power. Furthermore, not a few are horrified at the thought of giving money away at all. These are unfor-

KEEPING HEALTHY AND OBSERVANT

tunate fears, and to give in to them is to cripple one's chances of growth on the spiritual journey. Frankly, a look at one's checkbook will tell you a lot about the condition of the spirit and the kind of commitment that marks a life. A painful but true thought.

Just as God provides a discipline for the pocketbook, so he gives a sharpening effort that speaks to the issues of time and activity. This sharpening process we have come to call *sabbathing* in our home. Sabbathing activities include the pursuit of silence, solitude, renewal, and worship. In effect, God called upon his people to renounce their work for a day each week just as he seems to have called upon them to renounce a tenth of their income (see Exod. 35:2-3).

To neglect to renounce activity and work in order to pursue worship and renewal was then and is now to disobey God. Beyond that, our neglect of the Sabbath invites confusion of goals and purposes, decreasing our ability to sort out priorities and dispel the inner chaos that threatens our spirits. We were created to function *best* with such pauses. We place body, mind, and spirit in jeopardy when we avoid them. As with our money and our possessions, an out-of-control tendency surrounds our work that can begin to drive us. Some call this condition workaholism; others might call it being a driven person. Thomas Kelly was thinking of this sort of person when he wrote:

> In some we regret a well-intentioned, but feverish overbusy-ness, not completely grounded in the depths of peace, and we wish they would not blur the beauty of their souls by fast motion.[2]

The sharpening discipline of sabbathing is meant, first, to provide us an opportunity to look back upon our most recent *past* experiences. As we do so, we rejoice in God's grace, the value of our accomplishments, and the meaning of our work.

In turn, we offer up our achievements to God as an act of consecration. He gave us the skill and energy to do the work, and therefore our labor is really his.

God himself seems to have pursued this looking back during the Creation. Each day was concluded with a pause in which God surveyed his work and pronounced it good, thereby pressing value into it. Then, at the end of the Creation week, he paused again from activity and pondered the entirety of it.

Why would God take such a "rest"? Could it be that he wished to impress upon all whom he created that this type of appraisal and review was also necessary for us if we would be strengthened for the days to come?

Anne Morrow Lindbergh, not necessarily writing from a Christian perspective, nevertheless seems to have an intuitive grasp of this truth when she calls for a turning inward:

> *Women must be the pioneer in this turning inward for strength. In a sense she has always been the pioneer. Less able, until the last generation, to escape into outward activities, the very limitations of her life forced her to look inward. And from looking inward she gained an inner strength which man in his outward active life did not as often find. But in our recent efforts to emancipate ourselves, to prove ourselves the equal of man, we have, naturally enough perhaps, been drawn into competing with him in his outward activities, to the neglect of our own inner springs. Why have we been seduced into abandoning this timeless inner strength of woman for the temporal outer strength of man?*[3]

I'm reminded of the famous television commercial that highlighted the phrase "Where's the beef?" It is almost as if God is saying to us when he teaches us the Sabbath discipline: Find out where the "beef" is in one's past week. Is there any chance that an activity has been phony or tasteless? Has our schedule included value and growth possibilities? Has service been given with the quality of faithfulness? And was the Lord well-represented by our activity? These are Sabbath-type questions. They are hard and confrontative, but they sharpen us.

Pausing to sharpen our blades also permits us to ask hard questions concerning the *present*. What are we living for? What would we die for?

Out in the marketplace and even in our homes, we are beaten upon by ideologies that take their toll on us. Our values, convictions, and choices are often bashed about and belittled. Before these messages effectively bore deep into our interiors, we need to take the offensive and ask ourselves: What do we truly believe?

This, by the way, is one reason many churches have the tradition of having their congregations stand regularly to recite one of the great Christian creeds. They are reaffirming together what it is they understand about God and his mighty acts in history. They are giving witness that they repudiate the claims of bogus religions and philosophies that would seduce the spirit and dull the blade.

But our affirmation of the things we most truly believe ought not to wait for a congregational experience. We need to be doing this sort of thing—dare I describe a time frame?—every day. In this and many other ways, we tighten up our beliefs with the full knowledge that there are those "out there" who would like us to loosen them up.

We have clapboard siding on our home at Peace Ledge. As the sun and cold beat down upon the cedar siding, making it expand and contract, the nails gradually work their way loose. Every year Gordon has to go around the exterior of the house with a hammer, pounding down the loose nails.

As I've watched him make this annual inspection, I have been reminded that this is a picture of what happens to us during our "seasons" as well. Because our beliefs tend to become loose, we must nail them down before God and one another. That's what, in part, is supposed to happen on the Sabbath.

Then again, sabbathing helps us ask the questions that point toward *future* days. Where are we headed? What is God asking of us? How will we plan this week accordingly? Will our plans meet the guidelines of our purpose?

The manager might refer to this aspect of sabbathing as the planning function: Where are we going, and how are we going to get there? All of these past-, present-, and future-oriented exercises lead to a sharpened spirit. Having paused to sabbath, we are ready once again to get on with the work.

The ancient philosopher Amiel must have been thinking along these lines when he said:

> *We must know how to put occupation aside, which does not mean that we must be idle. In an inaction, which is meditative and attentive, the wrinkles of the soul are smoothed away. The soul itself spreads, unfolds, and springs afresh; and, like the trodden grass of the roadside or the bruised leaf of a plant, repairs its injuries, becomes new, spontaneous, true, and original.* [4]

In a world of furious activity and mind-bending noises, are we doing for our spirits what I see that farmer and his wife doing on the mountainside? Or rather, are many of us blind to the genius of the pause that sharpens? Are some of us condemning ourselves to harder and faster cutting because, as the blade gets duller, we think a greater volume of work is the only way to keep up the productivity?

Another question: Is it possible for us to retrain ourselves and others concerning the importance of such pauses? Yes, we have found it to be so. And history bears it out as well.

KEEPING HEALTHY AND OBSERVANT

Take, for example, Samuel and Susanna Wesley, parents to John and Charles, who placed the following edict on their rectory door:

> *Anytime in the afternoon or evening, the rectory is open for counsel and instruction. But only in emergency should the rector or myself be disturbed in the morning hours. Our family prayer, Samuel's study and writing, my own time of private devotions must be carefully observed.* —*Susanna*

For people who had to write their own textbooks, spin their own cotton, draw their own water, and make their own bread, Susanna's commitment to sharpening time was quite a feat. Her biographer notes that what the Wesleys discovered was that people in their congregation not only respected this value about the rhythms of "sharpening and cutting" but began to adopt their example.

We found the same to be true when we tried to teach and live these principles in the congregation. People needed someone to show them how to say no to good things in order to experience the best. Some have called it planned neglect. As Amy Carmichael once wrote to a friend, "Too much of your nature is exposed to the winds that blow on it. You and I need to withdraw more and more into the secret place."[5]

Just prior to the feeding of the five thousand, Jesus took time to hear the disciples report on their day's work. Call it a staff debriefing. Apparently Jesus saw the necessity of evaluating their work, too. Their recent pace had been intense. They had been flooded with people and their needs, and it's clear they were empty of spirit as a result. So Jesus led them into a little *planned neglect.*

> *"Come with me by yourselves to a quiet place and get some rest." So they went away by themselves in a boat to a solitary place.*[6]

Though the respite was short, the boat trip itself must have given them a much-needed break for sharpening their spirits. Even then, their performance before the five thousand people who awaited them on the shore left much to be desired. They were too tired to generate adequate care for the crowd, and they were too empty to summon the faith to believe it was possible to feed a group that size when hunger became an issue.

Perhaps more important than the miraculous way the Lord fed five thousand people that day is the lesson the disciples received and may never have forgotten: It is a terrible thing to become so dull that you not only become incapable of any more cutting for the day but you even forget that your essential purpose is to cut. When the situation calls for faith, the "dull" spirit says of others, "Send them away." The sharpened spirit says, "Bring them here to me."

The whole work of this life is to heal the eye of the heart by which we see God.
AUGUSTINE

CHAPTER EIGHT
The Sharpened Blade, Part 2

Gordon and I watch as the farmer and his wife return to their grass-cutting rhythms. Their scythes sweep the ground, and the grass falls uniformly in their path. I remind myself a second time that the work of cutting goes on with great efficiency because the work of sharpening the blades has been done first.

What happens when a man or woman determines that the discipline of sharpening the spirit will be an important part of life's regular rhythms? What expectations might they bring to the sharpening activities of sabbathing, worship, solitude, and silence?

Moses is a man qualified to help us understand the answer to these questions. A significant amount of biblical material focuses on his private sharpening encounters with God. A quick scan of it tells us several things.

First, Moses was teachable. He always seemed to be growing, and the central subject of his learning experiences was the *identity of God*: who he is and what his intentions are. Each time Moses learned a little more about God—for this matter of learning is a continuous process—it appears to have enhanced the development of a humble spirit.

In those sharpening times, God taught Moses many things. Among them: God's name and its significance, the history of his interaction with other generations, and his great pain over the plight of Abraham's descendants in Egypt. Slowly Moses acquired an awareness of God's plan for redeeming his people out of slavery and, in addition, a view of how Moses himself was going to fit into those plans. Each time, Moses left the presence of God more mature, changed for the better, obviously strengthened.

Through all of these sessions, Moses became increasingly aware that this God who reveals himself to simple people is an awesome and terrible God, One who deserves our keenest respect, and One before whom we must fall in worship and adoration. In his presence one does less talking and more listening. One takes off his shoes because when God is speaking, the ground itself becomes holy.

Equally significant in these sharpening encounters was God's attempt to reveal *the identity of the real Moses.* It sounds strange to put it that way, but the fact is that Moses needed much self-revelation. Like most of us, he no doubt carried in his inner life great distortions about his worth to God, about his own mission in life, even about his own personal capabilities.

If you've read much about Moses' past, you know that he'd been badly burned by a humiliating failure in Egypt. No doubt he thought himself to be something of a loser, a man who had acted hastily and violently for a noble cause only to be repudiated by the very people he intended to save.

So the man who stood before God by a bush in the desert was probably a man with a fairly low self-image. He badly needed to hear what he looked like from heaven's eyes: the

KEEPING HEALTHY AND OBSERVANT

good news and the bad news. It is this sort of insight—one's understanding of God and of oneself—that Sabbath experiences make happen.

The insights God gave to Moses about himself must have brought the man to his knees in repentance. He no doubt wondered why the God of Abraham, Isaac, and Jacob would ever draw near to him. After all, he was eighty years old, a murderer, a fugitive, a simple shepherd from the desert. Of what use could he be? Israel's future leader, God's prophet-in-the-making, would have appreciated what St. Augustine wrote: "God gives where he finds empty hands."

So after years of perceiving himself as a failure and a discard, Moses met God and heard of a mission that would involve him in the very areas of leadership he saw as his weakest.

This brings me to a third dimension that usually occurs in the sharpening experience of Sabbath. For when Moses encountered God, he received a *commissioning*. Frankly, the directives God gave him were not particularly welcomed. Moses quickly perceived that there were hard moments ahead, some that probably would far exceed his imagination. But in the hours of solitude, God etched a mission into Moses' heart and prepared him to carry it out. He sharpened him to become a man who was capable of loving, confronting, comforting, setting direction, sustaining, listening, absorbing, resisting, and arbitrating.

Isn't it interesting that the Father kept Moses with him on the mountain even though the children of Israel were perverting themselves down below? There's no panic. Only priorities. How easy it has been for me to rush to the aid of others in crisis without remaining in the presence of Christ long enough to receive the necessary filling. Moses was the prepared leader his people needed when he returned to the valley because he understood this priority.

Only God could have shaped a man to dimensions like

those of Moses; only God could have honed a man to a point of such razor-edged effectiveness. Later when Moses marched, he was no longer the reticent, reclusive shepherd of the desert. He was a man in control of his mission, his emotions, and his spiritual energy. He was indefatigable in his trust of God. Of course, he made some mistakes along the way. But most of us wouldn't have made it to the Pharaoh's palace for the first visit let alone to Mt. Sinai and beyond. Chalk up the success of his "cutting" to his willingness to be "sharpened."

I'm convinced that Moses' experience can be helpful to ours. As in his case, our times of sharpening begin with a recognition of who God is and, as a result, how much we fall short of his power and holiness. This latter awareness happens not to discourage or devalue us but ultimately to empower us with courage and instruction. Out of such a worship experience comes a renewed awareness that we are sinners in need of grace and mercy, that none of us lives beyond reproach. If we drink deeply of the gift of daily forgiveness, we are enabled to hear God's voice when he speaks in our lives. That leads, as it did with Moses, to commission. And for those of us who are in Christ, commission involves a sense of going out each day to enjoy Christ-like living as God has sketched it for us in the earthly activity of his Son.

But unfortunately, the plain truth is that most of us are not like Moses. We do not acquire the hunger for the regular sharpening of the spirit that he seems to have acquired. That's a painful fact. But if it describes us, we must deal with it.

If the farmer and his wife had left their sharpening stones back at the chalet or kept on swinging their scythes without taking the time to sharpen them, what would we have seen as we stood there looking up the mountainside? Simple: two very tired people for whom the work was becoming more and more difficult. We probably would have witnessed two people who, out of fatigue, no longer worked in the swift, concerted rhythm that a set of sharpened blades might make possible. And we would have seen uneven patches of grass as the cutting became ragged and haphazard. In short, it would have been quite obvious to us if the blades had been dull.

It is also quite evident when people who call themselves followers of Christ ignore the spiritual sharpening process. Let me describe what I sense are a few major symptoms of the unsharpened life. I mention these because they are also red flags I watch for in myself.

THE UNSHARPENED LIFE

Perhaps the unsharpened life can first be seen in the misuse of one's words. My homegrown title for the problem is *poor mouth control.* Listen to the words of any man or woman—the choice of conversation topics, the attitudes expressed about other people, the positive or negative perspectives brought to events, the effort made to encourage or affirm, the expressions of bitterness or joy. Over a period of time, these will reveal whether the condition of a person's inner life is sharp or dull.

While trying to avoid a morbid introspection, I make it a habit to listen to myself. For in the constant flow of conversation lies the possibility that the dark side of my being will gain control. If that begins to happen, it is a clear sign that it's time to take out the whetstone and get back to sharpening the interior blades.

I suppose one could control the mouth simply by closing it, never telling anyone what he really thinks or feels. But a better way is to sharpen the heart in the presence of the Father so that the mouth can be opened with the confidence that what comes out has been tested. The mouth simply "prints" what's in the heart.

The sharpened spirit connects to a mouth that speaks

kindly, that speaks sparingly, that speaks affirmatively, and that speaks respectfully. This is a mouth that speaks from a well-spring of communion with the Lord; its subject matter brings blessing to all who listen. Thomas à Kempis must have been thinking about this kind of speech when he said, "He who diligently tends to himself is easily quiet about others."

Second, I know my spirit is in danger of dullness when *people become my standard*. A red flag goes up for me when people, rather than the content of Scripture and the person of Jesus, become my standard for holiness. I am thinking of those times when I am tempted to feel unconcerned about an ungodly pattern in my life because I compare myself to someone whom I arrogantly conclude is "badder" (poor English but very descriptive) than I. One can always generate feelings of self-righteousness in the presence of someone who is obviously unrighteous.

My unsharpened spirit may also lead me to compare my choices with those of others. I may feel justified in making an unholy choice about something simply because someone else made a similar choice previously. Using these kinds of comparisons to establish holiness is dangerous and usually spiritually destructive.

We can play this unfortunate game in the opposite way also. The unsharpened spirit can draw us to someone who, in our judgment, is a remarkable person and prompt us to say, "I could never be that sort of person, so why try?" I suspect that this is as poor a way to justify low spiritual vitality as the other.

When I see the dangers involved in such people-comparisons, I quickly realize that I can never allow another person to be my standard for Christian living. I can learn from others; I can be encouraged by others; I can be prayed for by others. But only Christ can be the standard by which I measure my life and actions. An unsharpened spirit will not be discerning about all of this. It will not press us to the highest standard of excellence—Christ himself.

KEEPING HEALTHY AND OBSERVANT

May I suggest that a third mark of the unsharpened spirit is the tendency to fall into _whininess_ or self-pity. When I have neglected the sharpening process, I can see this negative attitude begin to quickly gather momentum. I can accumulate inner feelings highly sensitive to being let down by others, seemingly ignored by God, and left behind by circumstances. Or I can be tempted to dwell on a sense of being unappreciated and forgotten. Again, these are destructive responses, and they take a person nowhere but down. They are symptoms of a dull blade.

The unsharpened spirit can also be spotted in a fourth way: _overinvestment in tasks and short-changed relationships_. Busyness, achievement, and competition are all enjoyable pursuits when held in the proper perspective. But when they take us away from caring for those whom we love or whom God sends across our path in need of servanthood, something is wrong.

"Send the people away," the disciples said of the crowds.[1] It was a sure sign of their fatigue. About the time I'm tempted to be hard on these disciples for their blind spot, I'm reminded that I've said those words or had that attitude more than once myself. On each of those occasions, the inner "blade" needed to be sharpened.

We might discover that we also shortchange relationships because we do not want anyone near us who can spot our dullness. I've been engaged in one form of public ministry or another for many years. Usually I've found that it's not difficult to spot the person who has grown dull of spirit. They frequently avoid you, and when they can't, they keep conversations shallow and harmless. The truth is, when we're dull toward God, we're dull toward anyone in our circle of relationships who represents him. And so there have been times when people in that condition have avoided me, and there have been times when I've been aware that I'm avoiding them. In both cases—them or me—it's probable that the issue was an unsharpened spirit.

Inner deceit is a fifth evidence. It simply means that we have a frightening capacity to lie to ourselves about who we are and what we're doing.

There is an almost comical conversation between Moses and his brother, Aaron, when they meet after Moses' time on the mountain with God. Under Aaron's interim leadership, the people have erected a golden calf and worshiped it. Aaron is responsible and Moses is furious.

How did this happen? Moses wants to know. But Aaron is so dull of spirit that he cannot face the truth about the real events and what sparked them. His limp response: "I threw [some gold] into the fire, and out came this calf."[2] Moses must have been incredulous at Aaron's words. But they are an indicator that Aaron's spirit was too dulled to face the truth let alone speak it.

Deceit seems to pile up in a heart like rust on unpainted metal. It slowly strangles our capacity to deal truthfully about important matters. It causes us to lie to God, to others, and finally, to ourselves. When we sharpen the spirit, we are helping to prevent this from happening. That's what the psalmist was trying to say when he wrote, "Search me, O God, and know my heart; test my thoughts. Point out anything you find in me that makes you sad."[3]

Finally, I would like to suggest that an unsharpened spirit creates conditions in which a person chooses the course of *disobedience* to the laws of God. For those who have followed the Lord for a considerable amount of time, the pattern of disobedience may not happen suddenly but gradually. Each step away from the Lord's best is usually a baby one, and when the spirit is dull, one is not totally sure when the line into spiritually dangerous living has been crossed.

On most occasions, the disobedience not only hurts us personally, but it wounds many others around us who love and trust us. And one day we awaken to the fact that the consequences of an unsharpened life are difficult to hide.

I've often told the story of a little girl who got hold of a pair of scissors and cut away at her hair. When her mother saw her, she was shocked. "Mary, what have you done!" to which Mary replied, "I didn't think you'd notice, Mommy; I hid the hair in the wastebasket."

I smile but grimly realize there is a part of me that thinks similarly. Are we not all convinced from time to time that no one will notice or care when we have neglected the sharpening of the spirit? The truth is that we may often have a larger sign than we realize plastered all over us that reads: "I have an unsharpened spirit. My blade is dull."

RESISTING THE SHARPENING

Why have I felt it necessary to write about the sharpening and the cutting rhythm? Because time and again when I visit with people who have read what Gordon and I have written about solitude, silence, and sabbathing, I hear them locked in personal struggle. With their hearts they strongly agree: Without the sharpening experience (what in *High Call, High Privilege* I have called "fire times"), the blades of life get duller and duller. But their minds cry out that there's not enough time to get everything done in this busy generation of ours.

One says, "I can't find the time." Another is frank enough to admit, "It makes sense to pursue the pauses, but it's just not me. I wish it were, but I can't make it happen." Still another says, "I feel the need deeply, but I have small children," or "I'm a single parent, and time constraints militate against it," or "I live with much guilt about not doing this. Please help me."

In such conversations you know that a person is seeking some sort of breakthrough insight, a method or a tool that will make this sharpening exercise easier, even automatic.

They seek something that will make solitude, silence, and sabbathing a more desirable experience than any of the more immediate priorities in their lives. But that simply isn't going to happen. We are talking about something that is sensible but difficult, necessary but all too easy to avoid.

A recent television advertisement for athletic equipment attempts to help us see physical exercise from a new perspective. It frankly acknowledges that the effort of jogging, swimming, or pumping iron is sweaty, time-consuming, very tiring, and sometimes painful. There is actually no real glamour to physical exercise even if it's good for you, the ad admits, and so it simply concludes with a big, loud admonition, "Just do it!" And maybe, in the final analysis, that is the best word for all of us when it comes to spiritual discipline or sharpening: *Just do it.* For not to do it means duller blades in our external lives, and that's no way to cut grass well or live life wholeheartedly.

When I ask myself why I and the people I know sometimes resist the sharpening experience, I come up with some observations. I'm aware, in the first place, that sometimes we feel like we have failed so many times to establish a regular routine of meaningful sharpening moments that we are afraid to try another time.

Then again, there is a second group of us who would rather engage in things that are much more measurable than prayer, Bible reading, reflection, and listening. We prefer things that have more immediate results.

A third reason the honest among us might own up to is that it is discomforting to face the truth about ourselves. It's hard enough, some say, to deal with what I do know about myself. Who needs any more introspection (or "heavenly-spection") that adds more guilt or persuasion to one's already filled-up life?

I understand these thoughts because I think I've explored every one of them at one time or another. I understand the third group quite well. Gordon and I travel a good deal. One of the little things I don't enjoy about traveling is the flourescent lights in hotel bathrooms. They show up the pits and flaws in my face from years and years of pimple activity. I'd like to avoid the truth that the mirror shows under such light, but I can't. The marks on my face can't be denied. Scripture and the probing searchlight of the Spirit have a way of doing the same thing to the heart.

Could I suggest a fourth reason the sharpening experience is easy to resist? Let's be frank: All of us know lots and lots of people for whom life seems to be going quite well without time with God. "What's the big deal?" they seem to be asking us.

Sadly, the thinking of such people may mistake God's *mercy* for his *approval*. I honestly don't know how to deal with the question their life-style implies. But I do know that the men and women of Scripture and of the history of the family of God—people who offer life-styles and personal attributes I admire—had this one thing in common: They believed in sharpening, and they overcame great odds to make it happen.

Still others are uncomfortable with the sharpening moments because they find it difficult to be quiet. They have a restless spirit, an activist temperament. When I have visited with people struggling along these lines, I've identified with them, for I have spent many years overcoming the urge to be more active than quiet. Perhaps I'll work against this urge in me for the rest of my life. I only know that I have come to deeply appreciate the fruits of trying each day to overcome it. For when I needed the strength and rootedness such disciplined time before the Lord gave me, it was there to serve me.

F. W. Boreham in his little book *Shadows on the Wall* reminds us that everything in life draws us away from God, our anchor.

> *Every wind is against the anchor. The ship will go around with the wind, and the strain on the cable is the same whether north, south, east or west. Riches, poverty, success or*

failure—they all put a strain on the cable. All blow against the anchor![4]

Why drift when we can experience the fruits of being anchored? Or, to return to our farmer and his wife, why become dull of spirit when the sharpened spirit brings such rewards—present and future? It's our choice.

HOW TO BEGIN A SHARPENING PROCESS

Gordon and I have watched the grass-cutting farmer and his wife for several minutes now. They cut and sharpen, cut and sharpen, and the rhythm continues. We look at them through our binoculars. They are talking to one another as they work. You get the feeling they have been doing this kind of thing for years, that it is a routine they accept and carry out with the typical quality of excellence for which the Swiss people are known.

In our search for parables and pictures of spiritual truth, we talk about this cutting/sharpening rhythm and how one might write about it. It occurs to me that perhaps the greatest single obstacle for lots of busy people is simply getting started. Where do we start?

Perhaps we begin by admitting our needs and by opening up our lives. Thomas Kelly suggests that we begin with this simple statement, "Lord, I open my life to [you]; let me see earth through heaven's perspective."[5] Whether one has five minutes or ninety, to lift this prayer honestly to the Lord many times throughout the day can be most helpful.

Since we have spent much time on airplanes, many of our best thoughts come to us there. One day Gordon pointed to the flight attendant coming down the aisle pouring coffee for passengers. "Note how she does it," he said. I watched as

KEEPING HEALTHY AND OBSERVANT

the young woman asked each person to put their cup on her tray. Only then would she pour the coffee.

"I suspect she does it that way," I said to Gordon, "so that if there is any bump in the air, she won't run the risk of spilling on anyone."

"You're right," Gordon said. "But her routine also suggests to me something of how I have to put my 'cup' on the tray if it's going to be filled by the Spirit of God. You have to make the appropriate gestures. God awaits my heart's willingness; he will not fill it unless it's placed 'on the tray.'"

I know that is a tough task for a young mother who has babies demanding constant attention. And it's not any easier for the single woman rushing to work and trying to maintain a decent-appearing home or apartment. But then it isn't easy, either, for the woman in mid-life who is trying to balance a host of responsibilities and obligations. In short, every one of us will have more than enough excuses to avoid getting started if we want them.

François Fénelon, the notable French mystic, wrote a series of letters to a busy duchess in 1689. A portion of one of those letters sounds like he was writing to some of us:

> *You must learn, too, to make good use of chance moments: when waiting for someone, when going from place to place, or when in society where to be a good listener is all that is required;—at such times it is easy to lift the heart to God, and thereby gain fresh strength for further duties. The less time one has, the more carefully it should be managed. If you wait for free, convenient seasons in which to fulfill real duties, you run the risk of waiting forever; especially in such a life as yours. No, make use of all chance moments. . . . One moment will suffice to place yourself in God's presence to love and worship Him, to offer all you are doing or bearing, and to still all your heart's emotions at His feet.[6]*

So the busy life is not restricted to our generation. I hear Fénelon and others encouraging us to start slow and small. For instance, wedge out sharpening moments by rising in the morning fifteen minutes early, grabbing ten minutes from a lunch hour, focusing on spiritual matters a bit more during a late afternoon commute on a bus or train, or foregoing a thirty-minute period otherwise dedicated to television in the evening. A commitment to use the fifteen minutes before every bedtime might be a possibility. But we must find the time and get started.

There are dozens of helpful books on the mechanics of solitude and worship experiences. It is not my task to duplicate them. At the end of this book I've included a list of what I call snatch books. They make possible a little spiritual morsel-grabbing in various open moments of the day. They can help us to use effectively whatever sharpening time we have.

An important key is to recognize the loneliness deep within ourselves as a longing for God's presence. If we try to fill it with a possession or person or activity, we will be disappointed. There will naturally be times when we will be unable to observe our desired time of meeting with the Lord. At such times, think thoughts of *homesickness* rather than allowing the counterproductive feelings of guilt. The latter stifles, the former frees and brings renewed desire for the next sharpening.

One word from Scripture can carry us through the day if we will to keep it ever near in heart, integrating it into moments of activity. I am told that Ruth Graham used to have several books lying open in their home during the years when she had four very young children. The open book was more inviting than a closed one. She could snatch a nugget from it and move on to the next need that clammored for her attention.

It has been helpful for me to read Scripture thematically. Depending on what my perceived weaknesses are at any

KEEPING HEALTHY AND OBSERVANT

given time, I choose passages of Scripture to bring me into line. In this way I have explored such themes as trust or peace, fear or pride, anger or deceit, and stewardship or love. One reference leads to another, and I receive much helpful insight.

I've seen the bumper sticker that says "Born to shop." The slogan "Born to stop" might benefit us better over the long haul. Could it not serve a far greater long-term good if we would pay a baby-sitter to watch our children while we went apart for a time of inner sharpening than to pay one so we could visit the mall?

The farmer and his wife will always be a symbol of an important rhythm to me each time I visualize them on the mountain slope. They will go back to their farm home later that day with a strong sense of accomplishment. The grass has been cut for the winter. They have done it together, and they have done it properly—with sharpened blades that made it possible to finish the task with strength and excellence.

> *Oh, paradox of heaven. The load*
> *We think will crush was sent to lift us*
> *Up to God! Then soul of mine,*
> *Climb up! For nothing can e'er be crushed*
> *Save what is underneath the weight.*
> *How may we climb? By what ascent*
> *Shall we surmount the carping cares*
> *Of life! Which opes His secret stairs;*
> *Alone with Christ, secluded there,*
> *We mount our loads, and rest in Him.*
> —Mary Butterfield

CHAPTER NINE
Say Cheese!

The wanderweg from Langwies to the Strela Pass passes
through two tiny communities of summer chalets. These are
summer villages where Swiss farmers come to live for only
a few months. Beyond the chalets in the mountain pastures,
large brown Swiss cows graze. Here and there groups of
farmers cut feed, like the couple we watched earlier, stacking
it to dry so it can later be gathered into barns for the winter.

Almost every Alpine chalet is worth a picture. We have
been told that many of the homes on this wanderweg are
some of the oldest in all of Switzerland. The owner of one
told us that his was built more than four hundred years ago.
Yet as we studied it, it seemed to us as usable and durable
as if it had been built within the last ten years.

The quaintness of these homes, the brilliance of flowers in
the gardens and flower boxes, and the ruggedness of the
slopes on every side demand a camera. It is tempting to stop
every ten yards or so and photograph another scene. So as

we walk, one of us has the camera ready to zoom in with the macro lens on a flower or to zoom out into a wide angle on the line of a mountain peak that appears around the bend when the trail turns.

We have gone few places without our camera. It was with us on our honeymoon and with us when we brought our two children home from the hospital. We had it while we built our home at Peace Ledge years ago. And now on the path to the Strela it once again records large and small sights so we can possess a visual record of where we've been.

You could say we also do another kind of picture taking. It happens each morning when we rise and take out our journals to make a record of the last twenty-four hours of life.

Like many teenaged girls, I once kept a diary (something different than a journal) of my years in junior high and high school. Flipping through those pages thirty-five years later, I find it interesting to discover what was important to me then: a boy who was showing interest, a conflict with one of my friends, an occasional emotional low.

But I grew out of diaries as I moved through the college years, and it was a long time before I again considered that type of picture taking in my life. When the practice arose for me again, it no longer took the form of a diary. Now it was called journaling.

Gordon began working on a journal a few years after we were married. The discipline was prompted when he passed through a short period of personal disillusionment. A series of draining events had occurred in his pastoral ministry: a couple of tragic deaths where he presided at the funerals, intense busyness in the church, a lack of personal spiritual activity, the study of a book that virtually attacked the foundations of his faith. It all came to a head on a Saturday morning. For several hours he had a cathartic experience during which he was able to talk about how these events were affecting him. Together we worked through the feelings so that by

134

the end of the day he had regained his perspective.

On that very same day, a friend dropped by with a copy of a new book—a novel written by one of our favorite authors, Elisabeth Elliot, entitled *No Graven Image*. It was a timely gift, and one gained the distinct impression that God had used the giver to place in Gordon's hands the book that could offer the strongest encouragement.

The central figure in Elliot's novel was a young woman missionary, Margaret Sparhawk, who in the story passed through a personal crisis similar to what Gordon had experienced on that Saturday. Her moment of stabilizing insight came when an older, wiser woman said to her, "Margaret, what does God require of you but simply to do the truth?"

This powerful question became a major theme central to our thoughts. Doing the truth—regardless of the results, the opinions of people, or the rewards or costs accrued to us. It was a standard for planning, for identifying priorities, for answering those frequent questions that have no obvious answers.

But deciding to do the truth in life only raises more questions. When you are a busy, multigifted person who loves to help people and who tends to deny your own needs in order to meet those of others (not necessarily a virtue; just a fact of temperament), how do you maintain your perspective on what truth is? That's the next great question: What *is* the truth? Most of us might say: Show it to us, and we'll do it.

It was that set of thoughts that caused Gordon to become serious about journaling. He didn't want to repeat the momentary personal crisis of those days, and he knew he needed some device that would assist him in spotting the factors contributing to another buildup of negative energies. Beyond that, he wanted a way to record the good experiences so they could be remembered and, if possible, repeated.

A journal seemed to be the answer—a private workbook, if you please—a camera of the soul and mind that would provide a way to discern the truth and anti-truth. Gordon started journaling immediately and has kept it up for more than twenty years. It was not a fail-safe device, as he can tell you, but it was nevertheless a valuable one.

On the other hand, I saw little personal need to take up the same discipline. While he was naturally a man of words and loved to write, I was not. It was fortunate that he kept his conviction about journaling to himself. For if he had applied any pressure on me to do the same thing, I might have gone the other direction. But he didn't; he simply waited for the moment when I might grow curious about the benefits of such a discipline. It took ten years.

For many of us, the practice of journaling—this spiritual picture taking—develops when we experience a major trauma in life. For me that trauma came during the last few days of 1977 when I received word that my thirty-three-year-old brother was dying. I rushed a thousand miles to his bedside and sat beside him as life left his emaciated body. It was an unnecessary death. The tragic waste of life forced me to dig even deeper into spiritual resources for meaning and comfort.

That's when I turned seriously to paper and began recording the messages I received from the Bible, from loved ones, and from the depths of my own inner being where God was whispering. Recording these messages and my responses to them offered great solace. Feelings of hurt, even of anger, poured out on the pages. Affirmations of the eternal Word came to match them.

I had begun a journal. It would be a *memorial* to the work God was doing in my life; a *straightedge* to keep my heart from twisting into discouragement, deceit, or deviation; and a *testimony* for days of testing and trial that the sun would shine again.

How easy it is to forget God's many benefits. Whether by a memorial, straightedge, or testimony, all of us need help in remembering. The children of Israel were no exception:

"Then they believed his promises and sang his praise. But they soon forgot what he had done and did not wait for his counsel."[1] I began to discover what Gordon had learned earlier: The journal can be a magnificent aid when one seeks to explore inner space and discover the hand of God as well as the traces of evil.

As I've already acknowledged, people with certain temperaments or personality styles will be drawn more easily to journaling. But others will find it, at first, an almost impossible task. They will feel uncomfortable about putting their thoughts and feelings on paper. They will assure themselves that the whole world is dying to invade the privacy of this exercise, that people will line up to read their journals the minute they leave them unguarded.

Some will find it discomforting to see things pressed into words which, until then, had remained only distant impressions deep within. It can be frightening to force these feelings to the surface, name them, and determine how to control them. So we should not feel guilty if one person's enthusiasm for journaling is not immediately catching for another.

As I entered the discipline of journaling with increasing seriousness, it seemed important to me to find out whether the Bible had any encouragement for me. My first searches turned up interesting insights I'd never before pondered.

As God dealt with Moses, for example, he said to him, "Write this on a scroll as something to be remembered and make sure that Joshua hears it."[2] And a little later, when the entire nation of Israel had crossed the Jordan into the Promised Land, God again spoke now to Joshua, Moses' successor:

> *Choose twelve men from among the people, one from each tribe, and tell them to take up twelve stones from the middle of the Jordan from right where the priets stood and to carry them over with you and put them down at the place where you stay tonight."[3]*

The stones were to be a remembrance—a picture, of sorts—of what had happened at the miraculous crossing of the Jordan. They would be a sign to succeeding generations, and when questions were asked about the stones, the story of God's provision would be retold again and again (Josh. 4:1-8).

Israel's priests carried an Ark, an elaborate and very precious container, that held things to be remembered. A jar of the manna gathered in the wilderness was placed there as a long-term reminder of how God had provided for his people under arduous circumstances. Also included were stones upon which the Law had been written. These and other reminders were memorials of past experiences with Israel's God. When life had been grim, God had been faithful. I might suggest that the Ark was a kind of photograph album of great events in Israel's past in which God had miraculously intervened to bring deliverance.

The psalms seem to be marvelous examples of journaling. Many of them have a similar rhythm. They begin with a statement of praise or truth about the writer's God. This is often followed by the writer's feelings about what he struggles with, what his enemies may be doing, and what he wishes God would do about all of this. And usually they end with a reminder by the writer to himself and his readers that God is loving or faithful or just. Often this rhythm is repeated several times in the same psalm.

The psalms do not follow convenient outline forms like Western writings might. They are passionate, almost impulsive. They tell us much about what was going on in the hearts of real people. Some have called it pen therapy: talking to oneself and to God on paper.

Morton Kelsey, who has done much to encourage journaling, wrote:

> *The journal is like a little island of solid rock on which we can stand and see the waves and storms for what they really*

are, and realize how hard it is to be objective when one is tossed by them.[4]

In Psalm 73 the writer gave a magnificent example of pen therapy. He began with an affirmation of God's faithfulness: "Surely God is good to Israel, to those who are pure in heart."[5]

But even if he knew the truth in his head, he had to admit that, at that moment, his heart was not so sure. As he assessed his experience in the real world as of late, he had to confess that he felt let down: "But as for me, my feet had almost slipped; I had nearly lost my foothold."

And what's even more troubling, he'd been taking a look around and was troubled over the fact that people who were habitually unrighteous did not seem to have nearly the problems he had: "I envied the arrogant when I saw the prosperity of the wicked. They have no struggles; their bodies are healthy and strong. They are free from the burdens common to man; they are not plagued by human ills."

People who are impure, he went on musing, are rich, proud, conceited, hardened toward others, apparently carefree. If you can live like the devil and God doesn't seem to punish you, why be good? That seems like a reasonable and logical question, one not limited to the psalmist's thoughts.

But then the journaler went on to record: "I entered the sanctuary." There he found everything became refocused. He wrote:

> *"When I saw this, what tormoil filled my heart! I saw myself so stupid and ignorant; I must seem like an animal to you, O God. But even so, you love me! You are holding my right hand! You will keep on guiding me all my life with your wisdom and counsel; and afterwards receive me into the glories of heaven! Whom have I in heaven but you? And I desire no one on earth as much as you! My health fails; my spirits droop, yet God remains! He is the strength of my heart; he is mine forever!"*[6]

How clear it became as he put it in black and white.

Recently a man wrote to us to say that the daily discipline of journaling had helped him immensely on his road to recovery from drug addiction. His one-day-at-a-time struggle was encouraged as he came to his journal each day to deal with the truth about himself and his circumstances. How had he done that day? It was put on paper. Where were the temptations just ahead? It was put on paper. What had been the source of inner strength in those hours? It was put on paper.

Laying it all out on paper each day, he accumulated memorials to God's grace and power in his experience. As he saw his progress, he was encouraged to keep on an avoidance path that guarded him from the clutches of his addiction. Pen therapy works!

Adoniram and Ann Judson left Salem, Massachusetts, to be missionaries on the subcontinent of Burma in early 1812. They lived without a home and traveled constantly for the first eighteen months. Ann Judson had to adjust to living aboard several different ships, and the stress was enormous. But her journaling became a powerful tool for reviving her inner strength.

Finally on land for a few months, she wrote on May 6, 1813:

> Have been distressed for some days, on account of the gloomy prospect before us. Everything respecting our little mission is involved in uncertainty. I find it hard to live by faith, and confide entirely in God, when the way is dark before me. But if the way were plain and easy, where would be the room for confidence in God? Instead, then, of murmuring and complaining, let me rejoice and be thankful that my Heavenly Father compels me to trust in Him, by removing those things on which we are naturally inclined to lean.[7]

Do you hear Ann as a costruggler with the psalmist?

If Ann Judson's journal reflected great stress of the soul

during the voyage to the great subcontinent, it was to reveal even greater struggle later on, for circumstances in her life continued to grow more difficult. Because Ann was eight months pregnant as they boarded the ship for Rangoon, Burma, they had hired a European woman to help with the delivery. However, the woman fell dead on the deck just before they sailed, leaving Ann without any help when her first child was born. Weeks later when the baby arrived, it was stillborn.

Ann Judson's second child died at the age of eight months. For three years she and her husband received no mail from home. Nearly five years passed before they saw anyone confess Christ as Lord as a result of their efforts.

At one point it became necessary for Adoniram to leave Ann in order to make a journey to Chittagong. They agreed that Ann should stay to man the now-established mission.

Three months passed, and Ann heard nothing from her husband. To complicate matters even further, the mission's very existence was threatened. One of the Judsons' original biographers, referring to this crisis, wrote: "Nothing, indeed, but the special providence of God and the firmness of Mrs. Judson prevented an abandonment of the station, which might have been final."[8]

Another three months passed—still no word from Adoniram. Cholera came to Rangoon, and rumors of war between England and Burma began to circulate. Was any of this affecting Adoniram? Ann was left to her imagination.

She wrote in her journal:

> *How dark, how intricate the providence which now surrounds us! Yet it becomes us to be still and know that He is God, who has thus ordered our circumstances.*[9]

Then came July, the hottest month of the year. Morale among the people of the mission under Ann's temporary leadership reached a new low. Ann pondered taking the next ship to Bengal to search for her husband. But even that turned out to be impossible. Again she turned to her journal:

> *I know I am surrounded by dangers on every hand and expect to see much anxiety and distress; but at present I am tranquil and intend to pursue my studies as formerly, and leave the entire matter to God.*[10]

In a few days, Adoniram Judson returned after months of detours and storms that had sent his ship to India instead of home to Burma. How had Ann Judson survived the ordeal? I am convinced that God used her ability to express her feelings on paper both through writing to loved ones and through journaling to keep her from losing her equilibrium.

In the darkest moments of my own life, Ann Judson has been a friend with whom to commune through her writings. Ann told herself two things in her journals: first, this is how I feel; and second, this is what I believe. Both were equally important to her—and to me.

A journal should be broad in scope. People have written to Gordon and me inquiring about a system of journaling. They assume there is a process or a method. There really isn't. A journal should serve its writer. Into it should go anything that helps the journalist explore his own private and public world and come to terms with it.*

Charles Spurgeon once said, "People write their blessings in sand but their trials in marble." Better that both be written on paper. Thus blessings are not forgotten, and trials are not needlessly amplified.

When we take the time to write about trials and blessings, we are making a statement about life. In effect, we are saying

---

*See Bibliography for helpful books on methods and ideas for journaling.

all of life matters. God speaks not only in the beautiful moments but also in the painful. And he speaks not only in the large matters but through the smallest details.

Take, for example, God's instructions to the people of Israel when it came to making robes for their priests. He gave instructions that were minute. He even told the people to place seam binding around the edge of the neck to prevent the possibility of fraying (Exod. 28:31).

When someone first shared that thought with me, I was fascinated. What was the God of heaven and earth doing thinking about seam binding? This indeed, is a God who cares about details, I concluded. Into my vocabulary crept a phrase, "seam-binding moments," to describe those times when God seems to orchestrate the tiniest circumstances for our benefit and growth.

You see the detailed approach in Christ's instruction to the disciples after he fed five thousand people. Gather up the crumbs and let nothing be wasted, he said.

You see it in Creation. Some days after we climbed to the top of the Strela, Gordon and I made the almost obligatory visit to the Matterhorn. A guidebook informed us that around the Matterhorn, the local version of the common housefly comes equipped with "mittens and boots" (hairs in abundance), while in other climates houseflies have no hairs. Call it a seam binder—God's attention to detail.

You see it in the direction God gives to the smallest things done in his name. An Ethiopian eunuch named Ebedmelech is mentioned in Scripture because he did a kindness for Jeremiah the prophet. Ebedmelech had influenced officials to release Jeremiah from a deep cistern where he had been incarcerated. When it came time to pull him out, it was Ebedmelech who dropped rags down to Jeremiah to put under his armpits so that the ropes used to raise him would not burn him. Call it a seam-binding moment. The God of detail put it into the heart of one man to be concerned about another's armpits!

Why do I dabble in such stories? Because they affirm for me that one of the great joys in life is developing a sensitive eye to what God is doing, lest we miss it. Much of life is found in the details, and God is there.

My journal has assisted me in seeing the hand of God's detail in my life. I turn the pages, for example, and read of the time I left one of a pair of taupe high heels at a motel where we'd been staying. They were valuable to me because they could be worn with anything. And they were, after all, broken in. The minute we missed the shoe we called back to the motel, but they reported they'd found nothing. They took our number in the event it was found.

For three weeks there was no call. I was sure I'd lost one of the few shoes I really enjoyed. But something seemed to prompt me to make one more call.

The woman answering my call immediately recalled the lost shoe. "Why did you choose to call me this morning?" she asked. I informed her that it had simply crossed my mind to check once more.

That very morning just an hour before my call, three weeks after the fact, a guest had found my shoe lodged under the bed where none of the cleaning personnel had previously looked. But when the manager looked for my number to call, he could not find it, so they assumed they would never be able to locate me.

Who prompted my call at that hour? I noted this wonderful "coincidence" in my journal and called it a seam binder. Is God interested in details like this one? If he is concerned about a fraying neckline on a priest's robe, why not a comfortable shoe that goes with everything?

One evening as I sat at a banquet table randomly chosen from many others, I struck up a stimulating conversation with the woman sitting next to me. Before the dinner ended, she asked me about my plans for the coming days. I mentioned I was headed to a retreat the next day where I would be on the speaking team with a friend. Did she know her?

My new friend was incredulous. "You're kidding me!"

"No, I'm not kidding!" I said.

The lady at the table and the one with whom I was to be speaking the next day were long-time friends. Both were traveling at that time and were impossible to contact. They had planned to meet in a couple of days, but my tablemate had to cancel. Yet there was no way to send a message.

I became the messenger between two people who badly needed to be in touch. Both were extremely grateful. In my journal I called my part in the process a seam-binding moment.

My journal has scores of pictures like these. Simple, little "coincidences" that might otherwise have been forgotten— many of them extremely intimate and tender. When these "pictures" are placed into an album called a journal, you get a wonderful superportrait of a God who is ordering not only the major steps of our lives but also the tiny steps. Journals disclose that kind of information.

"My eyes are *fixed* on you, O Sovereign Lord. . . . When my spirit grows faint within me, it is you who know my way" (emphasis mine).[11]

These are the words of a journalist/psalmist who searches for the seam-binding moments in each day. He knows, as believers whose hearts are open know, that ours is a caring God. He is a God who walks with us in the furnace of life and gives grace and comfort that the bystander knows nothing about. Too often the experiences that remind us that God knows our way are left to fray, lost in a morass of activity, because we didn't take the time to write them down.

Someday our children will take the movies, videos, and slides that we have accumulated over the years and use them to reconstruct the memories of our family life. They'll see the pictures of our inexpensive honeymoon trip. They'll see themselves as infants on something akin to a bear rug. There will be graduations, sporting events, vacations, and even their own weddings. They will be able to visualize years and years of family experience.

But someday they'll also have our journals. And if they care to scan them, they'll see verbal pictures. X-ray-like, the pictures will speak of the high moments and the low, the exaltations and the deep, dark hurts. They'll learn even more about those times that Mom and Dad knew success and failure. And how God touched our lives in those difficult moments through the Scriptures, through our love for one another, through them, and through the encouragement of friends. They'll discover how journaling taught their mom to be open and transparent. They'll read about seam-binding moments they never knew about. They'll learn that we were real people who scraped through life doing the best we knew how most of the time. And they'll find courage for their own journey as they realize how much a God of grace empowered our climb.

If they turn many pages, they'll come to the day I was in Canada to speak at a conference. My hostess was the dean of women at a seminary, an older woman who had traveled through much pain in life and permitted it to press into her a remarkably Christ-like spirit. I had studied her throughout my visit and had learned much from her about how to respond under tension and stress.

My journal reveals how, at the end of the first day, I was greatly irritated because the meeting at which I'd been asked to speak that evening had gone on far too long. The next day was to be a demanding one, and no one seemed to be ready to get me back to my room where I could get a much-needed rest.

The next morning, after an unusually powerful time of speaking in which I felt God's strength substituting for my perceived weakness, I took a picture of myself in my journal:

146

I fought being on edge last night. But A—was total patience.
A silent rebuke to me. No word was spoken; she simply
manifested the Spirit of Christ. While I didn't verbalize any
anger, the body language was there, and the Father and I
knew. How could I possibly speak to others until I repented
of such immaturity? God, in kindness, moved today,
perhaps in part because he had Gail in a good place: broken,
needing his forgiveness and filling.

As we walk the path toward the Strela Pass, we pause
frequently. Gordon pulls the camera from his pack, and we
take pictures of things we think will be important to us one
day. There's one with me standing by a huge brown Swiss
cow. There are some lovely closeups of a curious purple mountain flower. And there's one we took of ourselves together.
Gordon simply put the camera on a rock, activated its self-
timing mode, ran to join me, and we smiled a lot and said
"cheese!" It's our very best picture.

Making
Pain
Your Ally

CHAPTER TEN
Down But Not Out in Dorfli

I fell! And I fell hard. The first pain signal was from a twisted
ankle. The second signal came from my wrist; I had strained
it as I tried to break the fall. And the third signal came from
the thigh on which I landed.

Our walk toward the pass had taken us through the tiny
mountain village of Dorfli, and just beyond the last chalet
the wanderweg turned from a one-lane farming road to a
rough trail. Distracted by the constantly changing landscape,
I'd failed to see loose rock just ahead. Without warning I lost
my footing, twisted my ankle, and was down instantly.

With pain coming from my ankle, wrist, and thigh, I could
feel my spirit of determination to make it to the top quickly
sag. For a moment the walk was no fun anymore, and it was
tempting to want to turn back. I had weak ankles anyway, I
told myself. What was I doing on this walk that was quickly
turning into an endurance march? No one had warned me
that the wanderweg was going to get this steep, and I wasn't

sure I wanted to risk any further injury to my ankle. Was it worth it to press on? To keep climbing?

As altitude increases, lots of not-so-subtle changes occur that affect the climber. Pathways grow more steep and rough. Winds blow vigorously. The landscape becomes treeless and rugged. Here on the path beyond Dorfli, only the grass, a few scrub bushes, and the tough mountain flowers grow. Weak vegetation and fearful walkers need not apply.

Falling is to the climber as failure and its consequences are to a follower of the Lord. A serious fall can take a toll on the morale of any one of us, whether on the mountainside above Dorfli or in the experiences of life. One is in danger of wanting to quit the climb.

Paul certainly must have understood this temptation. He had been stoned in Lystra, beaten in Philippi, bothered in Berea, and barely tolerated in Athens. Prolonged stress from persistent hostility must have brought fatigue, weakness, and discouragement.

That's what I see dominating the apostle's spirit on the fifty-mile walk to Corinth from Athens. And he's not helped as he enters that great city and sees the temple of Aphrodite, home of one thousand consecrated prostitutes, ruling the skyline. Before him in the marketplace looms a cosmopolitan city rife with sensualism, materialism, and paganism.

Where do you begin when you feel discredited, beaten, weary, and alone? Later, looking back at those earliest moments, Paul would write to the Corinthians about his first visit: "I came to you in weakness and fear, and with much trembling."[1]

It showed. Every indication is that Paul preached a defensive message in the early days of the Corinth mission. Gone for a short while were the old charisma and the offensive capacity to charge ahead and ignore opposition. Absent was the vigor that took on every opponent, caring little about what others thought.

When at first the Corinthian Jews resisted the gospel, Paul lapsed into anger and told them their blood would never be on his hands. He'd done his best, he said, and now he would turn to the Gentiles.

My own sense is that Paul was a man succumbing to the effects of long-endured stress, and there was a temptation, perhaps, to indulge in a bit of self-pity. Luke the physician seemed to think it important to let the reader know that even the great apostle had days when his perspective flagged.

I can't prove it, but I have a conviction that Paul may not have seen the seam binders God was piling up in his favor. Aquila and Priscilla were prepared to come alongside him and help. There was the interest of Crispus, the synagogue ruler, and his entire household, who later came to faith. But that wasn't enough for a man whose heart was wounded. He could only see what *wasn't* happening. And that engendered fear and worry. It's one of the only times it appears as if Paul's emotions may have been dominated by an adverse spirit.

Perhaps Paul's struggling inner spirit was not unlike that of Elijah centuries before. The great prophet, following a peak moment in which he witnessed the glory and power of God, was suddenly deflated by the threats of Jezebel, queen of Israel. He was so exhausted that he lacked the will or the energy to resist her warnings and fled instead to the wilderness. There, in despair, he told God that he was the only one left who cared about anything heavenly.

In response, God told Elijah, "There are seven thousand men in Israel who have never bowed to Baal nor kissed him."[2] This is the same assurance God was giving Paul when he planted these words in his heart: "Do not be afraid; keep on speaking, do not be silent. For I am with you, and no one is going to attack and harm you, because I have many people in this city."[3]

In both cases, Elijah's and Paul's, earth-centered tension threatened to crush their spirits until heaven-centered grace refreshed them. In both cases, God spoke tenderly to his men, giving them words of hope and comfort.

While staying in Corinth for the next eighteen months, Paul was able to regain an offensive stance, experience a powerful and fruitful ministry, and be free of physical harm.

I watch Paul moving from city to city on his own climb, and I marvel at his intensity. Because he loved Christ deeply and because he loved his Jewish people deeply, he was motivated to bring them together—to help Israel see its Messiah. Such determination could only bring heartbreak on certain occasions when his dream was not realized. Deep loving always brings pain.

This seems to be the risk any determined person takes. The more you care, the greater the pain when something does not go according to plan. I wonder if Paul was having second thoughts when he came to Corinth. Like me when I had a momentary flagging of spirit on the mountainside, Paul may have felt tempted to turn back.

"Prizing and loving [someone] yields suffering," wrote Nicholas Wolterstorff when he lost his twenty-five-year-old son in a mountain-climbing accident. As he worked through his loss, he began to realize that much of his pain grew out of the intensity of his love for his son.

> Love in our world is suffering love. Some do not suffer much, though, for they do not love much. Suffering is for loving. If I hadn't loved him, there wouldn't be this agony. This, said Jesus, is the command of the Holy One: 'You shall love your neighbor as yourself.' In commanding us to love, God invites us to suffer. God is love. That is why he suffers. To love our suffering, sinful world is to suffer. God so suffered for the world that he gave up his only Son to suffering. The one who does not see God's suffering does not see his love. God is suffering love.[4]

MAKING PAIN YOUR ALLY

Most of us are acquainted with a few people who have known various kinds of pain almost all of their lives. Obviously, there are those who live with incessant physical pain. Then there are others who live in relational pain, situations so ridden with acrimony and conflict that all of family life seems agonizing. Still other men and women go to work every day and do a distasteful job that they hate; but they are trapped, unable to make a change. And pain could describe the experience of not a few who have gone through bitter opposition and criticism from avowed enemies and critics for extended periods of time.

Today, after fifty years of life, I am no stranger to pain. I've met it briefly in the physical sense, the relational sense, and in the grief that death and loss bring. Gordon and I have known what it is like to be deeply loved by people, and we have also known humiliation. There were the high times in our lives when some who were struggling would say, "How could you ever know what I am going through?" But as the years have worn on and we have also accumulated the low times, we feel we can safely say to people who have fallen onto their own version of rocks in life, "I understand."

When I took that fall and twisted my ankle just beyond the chalets of Dorfli, I was strongly tempted to want to turn back. But the thought didn't last very long because, like Gordon, I wanted to see what the top of the Strela Pass looked like. Anything worth pressing ahead for is likely to include a little pain.

So after a brief rest, a tightening of the shoelaces, and much reassurance from my husband, we got up and started again. Perhaps our walking speed was a little slower for a while, but we kept climbing.

It has been important for me to study the lives of others, both in Scripture and in church history, to learn what helped them keep climbing. I've found some working principles that apply to those moments when one has sustained a fall of some kind—a failure, a conflict, a sickness, a humiliation, a serious disappointment, a betrayal. Are these throwaway moments in our personal worlds? Or are they growth moments, times we will remember someday as the greatest of our lives? To be sure, we probably won't ask to repeat the painful period, especially if we've dishonored the Lord. Yet, having said that, neither would we want to lose the depth of insight or the closeness of the grace of Christ that we have known.

In his most recent book *Rebuilding Your Broken World*, Gordon has written of many of the things God has taught us in our lowest moments. He writes of the counsel given to us by a life-long friend: "You have a choice to make. Fight or deny the pain, and lose all that it has to teach you. Or walk straight through it and let God speak to you in the midst of it. He whispers loudest in the pain." At the time, Gordon writes, we embraced the latter alternative.   As I look through my journal and see what I wrote during the moments when we allowed that awful pain to purify, these are some of the insights and principles that God seemed to whisper.

SEARCH FOR TREASURES IN THE DARKNESS
One of the get-acquainted exercises we enjoy using when we entertain new friends in our home is to ask a series of questions for each guest to answer in turn. The final question asks, "At what point in your life have you felt closest to God?"

I suppose I've listened to hundreds of responses to that query in our living room over the years. I am impressed that the majority of the answers focus on a moment when life seemed its darkest, when one passed through some sort of anguish or calamity. It was in that terrible time, many say, that God touched their lives with a promise, a personal insight, a sense of supernatural strength or courage. It's not unusual for someone to add that it was an encounter never to be forgotten and for which one will always be deeply thankful. What does that mean?

It probably means that our intimacy with the Lord reaches some of its highest peaks when we are at points of greatest personal need. We would never deliberately invite these experiences, of course, but somehow, paradoxic as it may seem, we often look back and conclude that without the pain, we never would have grown, never would have learned about grace, never would have gained the insights that later sustain us in even tougher, more demanding moments.

This is a principle that one probably needs to ponder and believe in *before* encountering any kind of significant pain: God desires to bring ultimate good and growth out of the most difficult moments of life.

The truth is that when we take a fall, the last thing we think about in the earliest phases is how good this feels or how much good can come out of it. No, our reactions are more automatic and usually negative. In fact, we may be overwhelmed by great agony or sorrow. If our fall involves sin and not just an error, the heart is likely to be consumed with self-loathing and a sense of hopelessness. The thought that God would ever give us a second chance in our tomorrows seems most unlikely. These instinctive reactions are not good theology, of course, but they're the natural ones, the way we're most apt to think unless we've schooled ourselves better ahead of time.

That is exactly why we have to train ourselves to a new view of pain if we are to keep climbing. We must discipline our minds to the notion that all pain can be a school in which one can learn. Paul wrote that pain is a time to receive the comfort of God in such a way that we will be enabled to comfort others when it's their time to hurt (2 Cor. 1:3-4).

Amy Carmichael points out that our Lord left us with that kind of comfort when he began to visibly suffer in anticipation of the cross, its pain, and its humiliation. In the garden prayer he said to the Father: "Now my soul is deeply troubled. Shall I pray, 'Father, save me from what lies ahead'? But that is the very reason why I came! Father, bring glory and honor to your name."[5]

Carmichael observes that *only one who prays that for himself can hope to pray it for others.* If relief, ease, and simple answers are our aim, then the prayers we pray for others won't do much for them. A fountain cannot reach higher than its spring.[6]

More than once I've watched a friend or acquaintance pass through a terrible moment in life—grief, betrayal, failure—and I've been impressed that such people frequently seem to possess a remarkable amount of serenity and determination in spite of the fact that we who stand by and watch expect a total breakdown. And why this expectation? Because we, the bystanders, imagine ourselves in the same situation and assume that we could not make it if it were us.

So the question comes: Why is such a person making it? Why? Perhaps the answer comes in the thought that the Spirit of God provides a special grace to the person in pain that may not be provided or experienced or even visualized by those looking on.

Onlookers at the grisly execution of Stephen, the first Christian martyr, might have been horrified at the pain he was going through as he slowly died under the rain of stones thrown by his persecutors. But Stephen seems to have handled the moments with remarkable grace. He even had the capacity to pray for his enemies. You could say he was drawing upon treasures in the darkness.

The Spirit of God infused Stephen with courage, with self-control, with an eternal view of life and death, and—perhaps—even a heavenly anesthesia that made the physical

MAKING PAIN YOUR ALLY

pain less important. This grace comes *only* when a person releases his will to God's purposes. And Stephen did that.

The other day I read about scuba divers who explore undersea caves and find magnificent beauty in sea life and natural formations. You couldn't get me that far down into the water, much less into an undersea cave, no matter what the persuasion. Nor, I will have to add, could you get me to take on pain voluntarily.

But just as the scuba diver has found treasures in the darkness of the deep, so there are strange and wonderful treasures found in the darkness of life's pain. As Isaiah wrote: "I will give you the treasures of darkness, riches stored in secret places, so that you may know that I am the LORD, the God of Israel, who summons you by name."[7]

In the days of my life when I felt darkness of a kind engulf me, I was acutely aware that each minute I was making a choice to either seek treasures or succumb to sadness. I recall now two special treasure moments.

A dear elder friend sent me a simple card that noted an inscription taken from a Cologne, Germany, cellar where Jews had been hidden during the Holocaust. It reads: "I believe in the sun even when it is not shining. I believe in love even when I am not feeling it. I believe in God even when He is silent."

For months I have carried that affirmation in my purse, pulling it out when I need a word of encouragement. It reminds me not only to pull myself together but to intercede for those who are unable to see anything but their present darkness.

On another day, a treasure came not in the mail but out of nature. Later I recorded my insight in my journal:

> *It occurred to me today that the boulders in my garden are*
> *a parable. They are too large to move, but I can surround*
> *them with flowers so that they become a point of interest*

instead of a (seeming) mistake. I know God often has flowers
he would like me to plant among the rough boulders of our
present pain. Will I turn them to his good or complain that
there is no way to get around them?

I can hardly think of anyone I have admired more in the Christian community than Dr. Helen Roseveare. Missionary-physician in the old Belgian Congo (now Zaire), Dr. Roseveare suffered terribly during the rebellions of the early sixties. At first it was only verbal abuse and harassment. Then one night the suffering took on a much more evil tone when she was repeatedly raped and beaten by rebels.

It is challenging to think about the supernatural power it took for her not only to forgive but to return later to that place and to those same people to continue her service in the name of Christ. That she would go back to a place of earlier horror became a badge of suffering that the people of the area greatly respected. And because she returned and forgave, a hospital was built, thousands were cared for, scores were trained in medicine, and the response to her personal witness became a hundred times more powerful.

In the years that have followed, Helen Roseveare has become a tower of strength to women all over the world who have come to understand that no suffering is too great not to be used if one is determined to find the treasures in the darkness.

Helen found one specific treasure at a period in her life when she was severely ill and had to be nursed back to health for an extended length of time by the people she had gone to help. Being a fiercely independent person, Dr. Roseveare was prone to resist the ministrations of the medical personnel she had trained to help so many others.

But her anxieties began to be allayed one day when her "disciples" explained to her that they felt closer to her than at any other time because now *she needed them.* At other times,

MAKING PAIN YOUR ALLY

she was the "take-charge" doctor who needed no one, they reminded her. This insight—that her helplessness was actually a strange and wonderful blessing for those who were treating her—became a treasure that Helen found in the darkness. It's frightening how easily that treasure could have been missed. And it would have been missed if she had permitted bitterness or haughtiness of spirit in her time of pain.

ACCEPT PAIN WITH OPEN HANDS, NOT FISTS

Was there a brief moment after my fall on the path to the Strela Pass when I felt angry with Gordon because he had chosen this path? If so, it was natural. For in our wounded moments, all of us would like someone to blame for our discomfort.

Pain tempts us to be angry at whomever we think to be the source of our problem. Perhaps that is why so many people get angry with God when they go through the pain of a loved one's death or the loss of a job or a serious illness. If God is such a loving God, one asks, why can't he take better care of me? Our thoughts are based only on how we are feeling *now*; they do not take on God's infinite view very easily.

It's easy to clench our fists and come out fighting. But no one will ever gain the great messages hidden in pain if they are "fisted." I'm not advocating that we invite pain in some masochistic way. But when the disconcerting experiences come, we open our hands, and instead of crying "It's not fair," we say, "Teach me, Lord."

Michael Quoist once wrote:

> *As long as a child plays quietly, his mother remains in the kitchen preparing dinner. But if he does something naughty*

and hurts himself, his screams will bring the mother running
to help him. Despite his behavior, she is there, more attentive
and loving than ever. But the child, nonetheless, can rebel
against his hurt. He can throw himself on the floor: he can
kick the piece of furniture on which he hurt himself: he can
strike out at his mother who is trying to help him. In that
case, he suffers even more, for his pain remains and
now he has to be in it alone—alone with his frustration
[emphasis mine]. But, if he loves his mother, he goes
beyond his pain and throws himself into her arms. She does
not take the hurt away, but in holding her child, she bears
the hurt with him.

In precisely the same way, we can choose in our pain an
attitude that further separates us from the Father or that
draws us closer to him. I guess it all depends on the posture
of the hands and heart. Amy Carmichael again:

Hast thou no scar?
No hidden scar on foot or side or hand?
I hear thee sung as mighty in the land,
I hear them hail thy bright ascendant star:
Hast thou no scar?

Hast thou no wound?
Yet, I was wounded by the archers, spent,
Leaned Me against the tree to die, and rent
By ravening beasts that compassed Me, I swooned:
Hast thou no wound?

No wound? No scar?
Yes, as the Master shall the servant be,
And pierced are the feet that follow Me;
But thine are whole, can he have followed far
Who has no wound? No scar?[8]

MAKING PAIN YOUR ALLY

AVOID BRINGING ATTENTION TO YOURSELF

When one feels the pain of some kind of fall, there is an overwhelming temptation to look around to see who is notic-ing and who will come alongside to offer attention. If they come, the temptation persists to reveal everything that is on our minds: our anger, our frustration, and our cries about injustice.

A dark part of the human spirit will claw for attention no matter what it takes to get it. And we can get such attention from some people if we cry loud enough. But what we get from people under the circumstances may cause us to forfeit what we could have received more importantly from God.

We must carefully watch our hunger for human sympathy when we're on the ground. It is not that a certain amount of it isn't right and good, but it does open the road to a kind of addiction to sympathy. Some have even learned to live on in pain because they have found it brings attention they fear they would not otherwise receive.

On many occasions I have talked and written about a young woman who was once like a daughter to me. I first met Lynn Schmacker when she was a young teenager. At first she was simply a baby-sitter, but as time passed, she became more and more of an elder sister to our then young children. From the very beginning, I saw unusual gifts in her when it came to communicating with and bringing out the best in preschool-ers. Now, twenty-five years later, I see dimensions of Lynn's personality stamped upon the lives of our adult children, Mark and Kris.

When Lynn left college, she gained a vision for investing her life in the rearing of emotionally damaged children as a foster mother. Sometimes there were six boys and girls at a time living in her home. Though single, she managed to provide the affection and security that every one of them so badly needed.

The state of Illinois child welfare agencies often entrusted to Lynn children who represented the worst abuse and trauma that could be inflicted upon infants. Since she became a prayerful woman, these children entered her home covered with intercession. And once in her home, they entered her heart. As they grew older, Lynn began the process of adopting six of them.

When Lynn was in her mid-twenties she was diagnosed with Hodgkin's disease. Year after year, when her physicians became discouraged about her chances to survive much longer, Lynn would rebound from one experience of chemotherapy and radiation to another. The children were her commitment to life, and she was determined to remain as their mother until each was officially adopted by her and would never again have to enter foster care. Obviously, she wanted to see to it that each had developed personality and character that would make them responsible young people as well.

Whenever I spoke with Lynn, I was impressed with the way she handled her pain. She suffered intensely through the years of her ordeal, but the casual observer would never have known it. She simply refused to attract pity in her direction. She believed that God would take care of her needs, bringing comfort directly or through a very small select group of confidants. And that is what happened.

If we could grasp the truth that Lynn possessed, we would not be tempted to be hardened by another's suffering as we often are. As I noted earlier in this chapter, we would see that God comes to comfort the one who needs it, not those who look on. We probably will not understand such comfort either; until, that is, we experience it for ourselves.

After a five-year fight, Lynn's body refused to go on any farther. Lynn accepted the nudge from God that it was time to surrender the battle and give her children over to others. Rarely have I seen such a championship performance as I did from Lynn, who quietly carried her cross and chose not to wear her suffering as a attention-drawing badge. She had an "affluence of soul" that had been forged on the anvil of affliction.

Lynn reminded me of Amy Carmichael's prayer for those who came to visit her room during the twenty years that she was bedridden:

> *If, in the paths of the world,*
> *Stones might have wounded Thy feet,*
> *Toil or dejection have tried Thy spirit,*
> *Of that we saw nothing.*[9]

So there I was on the steep pathway just beyond Dorfli. The smooth roadway back toward Langwies stretched down the valley behind me. It was tempting, now that I was in a bit of pain, to want to head back in that direction. But up ahead on the horizon was the first glimpse of the Strela Pass. My determination to get there overcame any signals coming from my ankle, my thigh, or my wrist. I was down but I wasn't out. A few minutes of rest, and I'd be ready to go again.

CHAPTER ELEVEN
Down But Not Out in Dorfli, Part 2

When we have sustained the cuts and bruises of a fall to the ground, whether it be a physical experience as on the wander-weg just beyond Dorfli or an experience of the heart in the greater arenas of life, we face a danger. We may become tempted to suddenly forget the big picture—what it is we're trying to accomplish and where it is we're trying to go.

Teresa Burleson puts this concern in words so delicate and descriptive that I would suggest the reader scan what she has written three or four times before going any farther.

> We ponder God's withholding
> or bestowing
> And while we pine for what
> was never given
> And what was taken,
> Today slips thru our fingers.

One rarely grows in stressful moments if there has not been an effort *ahead of time* to understand the possibilities of growth that are inherent in struggle and resolve to press ahead.

If I keep my composure while my ankle throbs and my wrist aches from my clumsy fall on the trail to the Strela Pass, it is because I've trained myself over the years not to strike out in anger or embarrassment. And while there's an instinctive urge from some point of childishness within me to want to blame Gordon for my discomfort—after all, he got me here—there is no purpose served in that. We committed to the walk together, and the matter of fault is irrelevant.

But the fall is a mirror of other falls in life that can be much more injurious. The question is: How does one act when one falls—or when one experiences the consequences of someone else's fall?

Here are additional thoughts to the ones I described in the last chapter.

LOOK FOR THE HUMOR IN THE PAIN

The talented Norman Cousins, in his book *The Anatomy of an Illness,* says that he beat serious illness partly through the therapeutic effects of laughter. He is serious about humor! His is not an entirely scientific explanation, but he is convinced there is an element to laughter that is medicine to the soul or the body in pain. I believe him, although I know it's hard to laugh when you're down. But it may be what we all desperately need.

A friend of mine who sustained a long period of depression told me she learned the therapeutic value of laughter through her preschooler. The child had fallen on her back in a mud puddle. Instead of crying, as her mother expected, the little girl looked up at the trees from where she was lying and exclaimed, "Look at the pretty leaves, Mommy." And my friend laughed. Perhaps one needs to ask God to send a view that looks up at the colorful leaves when we know we're in the mud. Humor is part of that process.

One of my "book" friends, Samuel Logan Brengle (now dead for more than fifty years) gave his life to the poor as an evangelist and pastor. One night in Boston, Brengle was accosted by a drunken, angry man who threw a brick at him and hit him in the head. The old evangelist was seriously injured and hung between life and death for several weeks. In all, he was incapacitated for more than eighteen months and endured periodic bouts of depression and headache for the rest of his life.

During the time of his recuperation, Brengle wrote a short book that was distributed around the world by the Salvation Army. It was translated into a score of languages and became a remarkable spiritual resource to hundreds of thousands of people.

When people tried to give Samuel Logan Brengle compliments for his book, he would simply respond, "Well, if there had been no little brick, there would have been no little book!" Mrs. Brengle seems to have shared his ability to smile at life's mishaps because one day he found her painting a Bible verse text on the brick. She told him she was beginning a collection of all the bricks that had knocked her husband down.[1] Their ability to laugh at themselves and life's jolts was an inspiration to me.

I once heard a woman who lived in another country comment on her experience of having her home looted after a hurricane. She said she knew her bitterness over loss was gone when, one day while in church, she saw a girl wearing a scarf that had been stolen from her and found herself laughing about it.

A friend who has taught me much about finding the humor in our misfortunes wrote a Christmas letter to her many friends soon after she chose a new direction in life, that of following Christ. Meg had experienced kidney failure the year before and, as a result, will spend the rest of her life needing dialysis at least three times a week. In her letter she wrote:

> Last July, when my kidneys finally pooped out, death came very close and seemed very real. But after my head was cleared of toxins, after I "came back," every day became a bonus—extra time.
>
> It seems as though I traded in a set of kidneys (which would have given out eventually anyhow, along with the rest of my body) for a relationship with God (which won't). So I have no reason to complain. I say that not as a stoic or a tough guy, but because if it took kidney failure to crack this nut—to lift the veil—then I thank God, very sincerely, for kidney failure. I must admit that if I had been drawing up the plan for my life, I might have been a little easier on me. Maybe I would have opted for flat feet or itchy skin or even the possibility of . . . anemia—something a little less dramatic—but "His thoughts are above our thoughts, and his ways above our ways." So, knowing the love of God, I go along willingly with his plan, and with C. S. Lewis, I am "surprised by joy."

Meg's humorous vantage point as she looked at the challenges of her life has taught me once again that we ought never to permit ourselves to get beyond the possibility of laughter. It is as important as the therapy of tears.

RENOUNCE OWNERSHIP;
THINK STEWARDSHIP
Gordon and I spent twelve of the best years of our lives in Lexington, Massachusetts, where he was a pastor. That

period of ministry came to an end when we concluded that it was time to leave the church and its people. It was not an easy decision for either of us, and perhaps it was hardest on me because I am by nature a rooted person.

In preparation for the good-byes I saw coming, I began what I called a "move journal." The journal, I reasoned, would be a place to deal with my feelings. I would record insights from Scripture and other sources with the expectation that it would prepare me for the trauma of the impending move. I wanted to make sure that when Gordon resigned, he wouldn't find me to be a drag on the momentum God was generating in leading us to a new place.

During this same period, I had been developing a Bible study for the women of my church concerning women in Scripture. As always, what we do for others usually comes back to bless us.

My study disclosed an important lesson relevant to my world. I saw that six women of the Bible who were major players in God's dealings with people—Eve, Sarah, Leah, Rebecca, Lot's wife, and Hannah—all faced one of two challenges. Either they were asked to leave their homes or they passed through a period in their lives during which they were infertile.

Being highly sensitized to the first of these by experience and to the second through a number of friends who were dealing with infertility, I reflected on the amazing commonality these biblical women shared. It was as if early in God's relationship with women, he wanted them to understand that he was Lord of the "move" and Lord of the womb. Having created us, he understood the pain we might feel in both situations.

Few things have been more important to most women than the opportunity to be mothers and to create homes and safe places in which to raise their children. So to permit women to face insecurity in one or both of these areas is to challenge them at the very core of their being. Yet this is the very thing that God permitted in these women's lives. I've also picked up these same themes in the lives of some of my favorite people in Christian history.

After five years of marriage and three children, for example, Catherine Booth, wife of the founder of the Salvation Army, wrote to her parents:

> *It appears that God may have something very glorious in store for us, and when He has tried us, He will bring us forth as gold.* My difficulty is in leaving home.[2]

Of the great missionary, Mary Slessor, her biographer wrote:

> *On the night before she left home to go, not overseas, but only to Edinburgh for her course . . . the woman who would one day be described as "a tornado" crept down to the door of the lobby of the tenement building where she lived and cried her eyes out.*[3]

When Amy Carmichael prepared to leave England for Japan, where she had her first missionary experience, people thought her a hero. Only she seemed to know that in her heart she was in deep personal pain. She wrote:

> *They think I* want *to go. If they only knew how torn in two I feel today, and how precious the home ties are, they would understand. . . .*[4]

When I study the Bible's women and try to appreciate what their feelings must have been, I am comforted to know that God is not silent or unfeeling about them—or us. Like them, we are heard and we are understood. But this comfort comes only when God is given the title deed to our lives and permitted to take our pain and turn it into a growing experience.

MAKING PAIN YOUR ALLY

Sandwiched in among the six is one woman, Lot's wife (whose name we do not know), who fought the move out of Sodom. She dug in her heels all the way and then, on the way out, looked back. The woman had become attached to the "stuff" of her home, and as a result, she lost everything, even her own life. When I was in the midst of pondering what it might be like to leave my home in Lexington, I read of her calamity and got the message very quickly. Lot's wife had tried to hold on to things that had never really belonged to her.

In Gordon's book *Ordering Your Private World*, he pictured John the Baptizer as the consummate model of the called man, a contrast to what he called the driven man. John's attitude of "calledness" is seen clearly in the latter days of his public ministry when the crowd that had come so often to hear him suddenly drifted away to listen to Jesus. You could say that John was suddenly losing his job.

It could have been a crisis. How would he handle such a thing? When asked what he thought about all the people going toward Jesus, John said, "A man can receive only what is given him from heaven."[5] His point was that everything he'd had to date was purely on loan from the one who had placed it at his disposal. Who was he to question when what was loaned was taken back?

As I wrote each day in my "move" journal, I began to think of the group of women I'd been privileged to lead and train as being on loan to me. Now God was going to take them back and team them up with someone else.

At the same time we were preparing to break up our memory-filled Lexington, Massachusetts, home, our children were coming to the point of saying their good-byes to family life and leaving for college and adulthood. They too had been on loan to their father and mother. The ministry we had enjoyed for twelve years, the home we had loved, and the children who were so much a part of our beings—none of them were ours! And if we had assumed the way of the owner, we would have drawn much needless pain to ourselves.

Thomas à Kempis put it this way:

> *Whenever a man inordinately desires anything, he instantly loses inward peace. The proud and covetous are never at rest, while the poor and lowly in spirit pass their life in continual peace.*

In preparing for the day when Gordon and I would leave our home and our children would leave us, I enlisted friends who knew of my reluctance to change and let go. I asked them to pray that I would have an inner release from needing to have a life of routine and permanent relationships—and that my poor attitude about "suitcase living" would dissolve. These things had to be prayed for and dealt with *in advance* so that when the time came, the changes could be managed.

Corrie ten Boom spoke of her dislike for the living-out-of-a suitcase life-style when she wrote:

> *I had the spirit of resentment. I started to argue when I remembered that Jesus cannot cleanse an excuse; so I confessed my sin and told the Lord that I was willing to do whatever he had for me.* [6]

When the time of our move arrived, I discovered that God had heard my prayers and those of my friends. He caused me to realize that he had come to make *his* "home" in me and that I could go anywhere and have the assurance that he would precede me. I came to see that what I would lose when we left Lexington was never mine anyway, and that the children we had raised had been raised to one day leave and fulfill God's purposes for them. Thank God, they frequently come back. By slowly learning to renounce ownership and think stewardship, I came to discover that one never really loses anything.

TAKE NO CREDIT FOR "CARRYING" GRACE WHEN IT IS GIVEN

For a short time after my fall on the pathway, Gordon and I rested. But then it was time to try again. Every step for the next little while was painful. Gordon looped his arm through mine, lifting me half off the ground, to lessen the weight on my turned ankle. We were going to keep climbing— the both of us—even if I had to be dragged. I think he would have carried me if it had been necessary. We simply wanted to keep going.

Being carried. Theologians often may specify several types of grace when they speak of the redeeming and sustaining God of the Bible. I wonder if they would be comfortable with the concept of carrying grace—where one lifts another and helps to relieve the pain. There are marvelous biblical pictures of the God of carrying grace. Is there any greater picture than the one that features Christ, the Good Shepherd, carrying the lost sheep out of the wilderness and into the sheepfold?

Isaiah presents us with a picture of the God of carrying grace when he records this message from heaven to Israel:

> *I have upheld you since you were conceived, and have* carried *you since your birth. Even to your old age and gray hairs I am he, and I am he who will* sustain *you. I have made you and will* carry *you* [emphasis mine].[7]

This is the same heavenly Father who comes alongside when we are weak and carries us until we are strong again. He is consistent in his treatment of his people for all time.

Sophie de le Haye and her husband, Ray, were Christian missionaries in West Africa for more than forty years. In her latter years, she suffered from a rare muscle disease that caused her to lose all motor control in her body. This once-strong, independent-minded woman, who had lived in some of the most rigorous parts of Africa and had withstood stresses most of us will never see in a lifetime, was suddenly reduced to a point where she could not even lift a cup to her mouth or button her clothes.

When Sophie frequently came to those moments of utter helplessness, she would stop, she told me, and simply say, "For *this* you have Jesus." Somehow this simple affirmation helped her figure out a way to do what she needed to do or relax until someone else came to her aid. Sophie never seemed to lose her smile even though she had lost a great deal of control over her body. It is impossible to say how full of courage and hope her letters to me were right up until the month she left us for heaven.

Sophie rejected the soft road; she resisted self-pity. Rather than permit our conversations to center on her and her infirmities, she always managed to direct the subject to Christ. He was the empowering One, she said, and it was her hope that I would always remember that. I learned more about carrying grace from her than anyone I've ever known. And it was she who made sure I knew where the grace came from.

Months before she died, Sophie arranged to send me her much-marked copy of Amy Carmichael's *Gold by Moonlight*. I was entranced as I read not only the words of Carmichael but the notes in the book's margin that Sophie had jotted there over the years. It was as if the two women had had a conversation: Amy initiating, Sophie responding. I imagine that by now they have met in heaven and engaged in some rather long dialogues.

Amy quoted Paul: "None of these things move me, neither count I my life dear unto myself, so that I might finish my course with joy." In the margins next to that Pauline reference, Sophie wrote simply, "Yes, Lord."

In Sophie's copy of Carmichael's book, the following passage is underlined several times. Perhaps it meant the more to Sophie because of the picture of a mountain on the opposite side of the page. The rock, or mountain, only shone because the sun's "spotlight" was on it.

He shines upon his dust and the dust shines! There is no light in the rock. But it is bathed in light. In a picture it is the light that makes the difference. So when my thoughts shine, I can know that I have been shined upon! It is of no account that we are nothing. He shines upon his dust, and his dust shines. If, however, there is dimness, is it because we see too much of man and not enough of the Master?[8]

For any of us who have fallen, carrying grace becomes a major issue. And it is this carrying grace that should be celebrated, not the one carried. Without it, we fallen ones would simply remain immobilized where we stumbled. Without it, we would eventually turn back, quit climbing. But this carrying grace of God lifts us to our feet and helps us take our first tentative steps forward again.

One day I sat at an airport gate waiting for a flight. A small child ran back and forth among the passengers. Suddenly he tripped and fell, his forehead taking the brunt of the blow. When he looked up, his eyes, already wet with tears, sought out his mother's face. She came toward him, and his arms reached out, seeking her closeness. She picked him up and let him sob out his pain and maybe his embarrassment on her shoulder.

Hers were the motions of carrying grace. As she toted him on her shoulder, he was *unable to see where he was going, only where he had been,* but he nevertheless trusted in her ability to carry him safely. He might not have called it carrying grace, but he surely accepted it. A beautiful picture, I think, of our relationship to our heavenly Father.

If we, like others who have known pain, are intact today with a heart's desire to serve; if Gordon and I walk together, our relationship more deeply welded than ever; if we have a sensitivity toward those who are falling in a hundred ways, it is not because of anything in us. We have simply received grace. We take no credit for it. How can you boast about a gift?

WHEN MISUNDERSTOOD, NEVER FIGHT BACK

No principle has meant more to us or challenged us more than this one. It is, as I have mentioned earlier, instinctive to want to preserve one's self. Yet if we have come before the Lord in brokenness and done those things he requires to show the fruits of repentance for any wrongdoing on our part and are still misunderstood, we must hear what Amy Carmichael heard the Lord whisper to her heart at such times: "Let it be; leave it to Me; think of Me."

And to him respond: "My times are in Thy hand. . . . My God, I wish them there."

And to ourselves:

> [Don't] weigh flying words, or let [our] peace be in the mouths of men. . . . If He remembers, what does it matter that others forget?
>
> We can thank Him for all who trample unawares upon us, talking smooth nothings. For we know, just because they can do it so unconsciously, so easily, and with so airy a grace, that they, at least, were never laid in iron; and is that not good to know? [emphasis mine].[9]

When our Savior was standing before his accusers, they tried to get him to fight back. "Aren't you going to answer? See how many things they are accusing you of!" But his only reply was one of holy stillness. In contrast, St. Augustine spoke for most of us who would like to explain ourselves to every critic and every accuser. He said, "Lord, deliver me from the lust of always vindicating myself."

Those who know me well are aware that one of my favorite people in church history is Catherine Booth. Her husband, William, the founder of the Salvation Army, was often slandered and criticized. But when the raw and biting comments of mainline religious leaders were directed at Catherine, William found that more difficult to accept than anything that had ever happened to him. His challenge to Catherine in that moment is powerful.

> *I cannot understand how they can possibly treat you and the work of God thus. If it had been me, I should have scarcely marvelled, but you—it is absolutely confounding. . . . I am sure I hardly know what to advise. That which comes first is give them up and do it with a high hand. Then second thoughts say that ten years hence the treatment we personally receive from these "leaders" (in religion) will be as NOTHING. We shall all but have forgotten it.* But our treatment of the work of God, our forbearance and humility and meekness and perseverance *under and in the face of difficulties will be* everything.[10]

The choice not to fight back is at least part of the reason the Salvation Army has continued to be a light to the suffering for so many years. To have made lesser choices and pursued vindication would have brought momentary relief to the Booths but not long-term growth and inner well-being. We must not underestimate what it has meant to succeeding generations of Army people who learned by their leaders' precedent.

The Booths brought out the best in one another. To have a close relationship—marriage or friendship—that helps you master yourself is a gift beyond measure. It is an important thing to have friends and loved ones who will encourage us in our desire to rise above the vindictive sickness of this age in which the words *me* and *my* seem supreme. We live in a time of court suits, getting even, hurting indiscriminately, anonymous letters, telling all, profaning all. We can ill afford to get tangled up in it. To lower ourselves to such behavior is to risk losing our soul's health in the process.

François Fénelon's words have often moved me:

> *Let yourself be humbled; calm and silence under humiliation are a great benefit to the soul. One is sometimes tempted to talk humility, and it is easy to find plenty of opportunities for so doing, but it is better to be humbly silent. Talkative humility is always suspicious; talk is a certain relief to self-conceit. Do not get angry about what people say; let them talk while you try to do God's will. As to the will of men, you could never come to an end of satisfying it, nor is it worth the trouble. Silence, peace, and union with God ought to comfort you under whatever men may falsely say. You must be friendly to them, without counting on their friendship. They come and go; let them go—they are but as chaff scattered by the wind.*[11]

Years ago, Bishop Whipple worked at being that kind of friend when he said: "For thirty years I have tried to see the face of Christ in those with whom I differed." Each generation has faced this challenge. They and we will climb higher when we remember to do this: "Consider *him* who endured such opposition from sinful men, so that you will not grow weary and lose heart" (emphasis mine).[12]

CONTRIBUTE TO ANOTHER'S JOYS

In my study of the sufferings of Jesus, I have been challenged to realize that his pain began long before the cross. The anticipation must have magnified his suffering greatly. Yet during that agonizing countdown toward Calvary, Jesus seems to have managed the stress by giving himself to others.

There is great genius to the notion that one's pain becomes more manageable when he disciplines himself to encourage

MAKING PAIN YOUR ALLY

joy in others. This is among the toughest of disciplines, one that demands great tenacity of purpose. But it works! I've seen it work in the life of a woman I have always highly admired and loved.

My Aunt Georgia was a teacher of handicapped children. Because she lived not far from my girlhood home, I saw her frequently. I grieve now that as a young girl I took her for granted. When Aunt Georgia was alive, it never dawned on me to ask her why she had chosen the single life or why she had made a commitment to the handicapped people of her generation. Only after I had long left my birth home, was married, and began to reappraise my family roots did I begin to uncover Aunt Georgia's unusual story of personal honor and valor.

Why was Aunt Georgia single? The fact is she hadn't been. She was a widow. Georgia Scott had married Walter Dickens, a railroad train conductor, many years before I was born. After several months she became pregnant, and the two of them began to anticipate the coming of their first child.

The happy home Georgia and Walter envisioned was not to be because their baby died soon after birth. But that was not the end of my aunt's tragedy. For while she was still in the hospital recovering from the delivery, Aunt Georgia was notified that Walter had been killed in a train accident. Question: How does one put life back together after a double blow of this magnitude? How does one manage such intolerable pain?

For Aunt Georgia, the answer came in the pursuit of this principle: She determined to contribute joy to others. Some of the special benefactors of that determination were my parents, then newly married. Because she had a small nest egg, Georgia assisted my mother and dad in the purchase of their first home with a no-interest loan. Then she returned to school, majoring in special education, a relatively new discipline in public schooling. In my files I have her first teaching contract, which offered Aunt Georgia $750 a year to teach the handicapped children of the Aurora, Illinois, school district.

For the next thirty-five years Georgia taught twenty handicapped children a year. When she retired, scores of people came to pay her honor. When I read the description of all those who praised this quiet, determined woman, I asked myself what the Aurora community would have done if my Aunt Georgia had rebelled against her pain instead of determining that her life would contribute to the joy of others.

When I play back in my mind the family pictures of my Aunt Georgia, I realize her role in our lives was that of "being there" and celebrating our great moments—a graduation, a wedding, the coming of a child. But never do I remember a word about her loss of many years before. Never a recollection of what might have been. Never an attempt to play the martyr or to put a damper on the joy of someone else's special moment. What must have gone through her mind as she celebrated each of our family milestones? Did she ever quietly visualize what it would have been like if those occasions had been held for her and her long-ago husband and child? If she did, we never knew it. She was simply caught up in our excitement.

A pearl, I'm told, is a wound healed. No wound, no pearl. It has been said that whether life grinds or polishes us depends upon what we are made of. I know now that Aunt Georgia's daily choice to contribute to the joys of others was no small thing. She had allowed her life with its broken pieces to become a thing of beauty for all of us.

In her book *Thank You, Lord, for My Home,* Gigi Tchividjian writes of a day when her mother, Ruth Graham, visited the shop of a man who specialized in piecing broken pottery and china back together. It was Mrs. Graham's wish to buy something with one piece missing. When the craftsman showed surprise, she explained to him that his activity reminded her of God's work in human life. God, she said, "carefully and lovingly takes the broken pieces of our lives and glues them back together again."[13]

Here and there, all of us have missing pieces: Someone has died; there has been a divorce; someone has done wrong and brought us pain as a consequence; a long illness has left enduring weakness or discomfort. Still, God glues us back together. The cracks and holes will remain until someday in eternity they are restored to their intended beauty.

Aunt Georgia is gone now, and all the pieces are back in place for her. But while she lives in heaven, she lives also in my heart, a reminder of a woman who kept climbing in spite of a terrible, terrible fall. She turned her pain into great gain.

I have fallen hard on the pathway beyond Dorfli. I am tempted to be angry at myself for being less than diligent. I'm tempted to be angry at Gordon for getting me into this. And I'm tempted to be angry at those dumb rocks.

But those temptations are soon gone. The outline of the Strela Pass is on the horizon, and we may not come this way again. The pain in my ankle will go away. Gordon's arm and a stick will give me a bit of strength until I'm ready to walk on my own in a few minutes.

Amy Carmichael writes in poetry form:

> *Make me Thy mountaineer;*
> *I would not linger on the lower slope.*
> *Fill me afresh with hope, O God of hope,*
> *That undefeated I may climb the hill*
> *As seeing Him who is invisible.*[14]

Again, Sophie de le Haye, having read this poem, has marked her copy of Amy's book in the margins with "Yes, Lord." What pain was Sophie feeling at the moment when she scrawled that affirmation next to Amy's written determination? What heartbreak was she facing? What fear was she fighting? Or what temptation was she resisting? Whatever it was, Sophie was still climbing.

And so am I. I'm not going to give up now. The pain of my fall on the wanderweg has sharpened my senses; I'll be more careful. And we will keep climbing.

CHAPTER TWELVE
The Comforter-Friend

For some distance, the pathway to the top of the Strela Pass
follows the floor of a long, curving mountain valley. At each
turn are markers to give the walker his next heading.

Sometimes the markers are signs—a yellow painted arrow
with the name of the destination and an estimate of the time
it will take to reach there. These yellow signs are standard in
size and appearance and are familiar to all who have walked
or skied the Swiss *wanderwegs*. Sometimes there is a special
mark—usually three parallel stripes—in painted bright colors
on prominent rocks. The walker learns to look for the yellow
signs and the marked rocks all along the way. It's too easy to
stray off course otherwise.

On the way to the pass, there comes a point when you
realize that the path has left the clusters of farmers' homes
in Dorfli and Sapun far behind. Now it seems as if there are
nothing but high-rising mountain walls that are coming closer
and closer together as if to form a canyon. Soon they will

force a stiff final climb up the side. About the time you are sure you will see no further life until you reach the top of the pass, you come over a rise and see one more chalet. The walkers' map has the location marked and identifies it as the Berghaus Heimeli, owned and operated by the Swiss Familie Merki.

The Berghaus is a three-floor chalet open to hikers in the summer and skiers in the winter. It's typical of the mountain inns one finds throughout the Alps. Now, some of them are rather Spartan places—simple, large rooms with a dozen or more beds lined up against the walls where tired hikers can collapse for a night of sleep after an evening of food and singing. Not much privacy, but I'm not sure exhausted people care that much. Others, like the Berghaus Heimeli, are a bit more comfortable; you will find individual rooms and a few more of the indoor conveniences to which American middle-agers are accustomed.

There are centuries of tradition behind these mountain inns. Long-distance walkers have knocked at their doors for as long as they have traversed the length of Switzerland. The books on walking say the proprietor of a mountain inn will never turn away a mountain walker at night, even if the inn is already filled. He will find one more place to take in a straggler, even if someone has to sleep on the floor. It would be unthinkable to turn someone away at night. As everyone is aware, the mountains can become quite dangerous when evening comes.

As we approached the Berghaus Heimeli, we could see tables and chairs set outside on the deck in the sun. It was time for a midmorning pause and something cold or hot to drink. Soon the innkeeper was serving us hot coffee and some of the bread and cheese one finds everywhere in the Alps. What a refreshing, safe place, this *berghaus* high in the mountains with its incredible view and its friendly owner who comes from the kitchen with a repast to revive the tired walker.

The innkeeper knows the mountain better than anyone. He is the first one to spring into motion if a hiker falls and is hurt or if a skier is injured. He is not there to make you feel like an intruder or to tell you what you can or can't do. He gives advice when asked, hospitality when visited, an energetic conversation when engaged. He is the cheerleader and the direction-giver on the high mountain path, and it's wise to make his acquaintance.

The innkeeper symbolizes something I've come to call the comforter-friend, a person who occasionally comes along the pathways of real life. In innkeeper's language, the comforter-friend is that person who opens the door and bids the traveler to come in on a day or a period in life when one is exhausted, when one has taken a bad fall, or when one is vulnerable to the onset of darkness.

The comforter-friend is a unique person, and any of us who have passed through a time of personal suffering can name one or two (perhaps a few more) who have known how to transfer hope, value, and strength just when we thought we had exhausted our own reserves.

Gordon and I have had to learn how to be comforter-friends to one another. I think about that when I take a couple more falls on the trail. I fall, I realize, because the shoes I'm wearing are not appropriate for this mountain terrain. Gordon had warned me about that several times in previous days. He had insisted that we purchase a pair of hiking boots for me, but I had resisted, worrying too much about price and the right color and my general tendency not to want to buy "frivolous" things.

But now my occasional slips on loose rock are proving Gordon right. I should have bought the boots when I had a chance. Now my fear of slipping is putting a damper on my ability to enjoy this part of the walk.

When I fall a third time, I'm impressed with the fact that Gordon says nothing about my inadequate shoes except to ask if he can help. "Do you want to head back?" he asks. I know he'd be disappointed to do so, but it's clear he'd do it without a word if I said yes. I'm grateful he doesn't complain about my earlier refusal to buy what he said was necessary.

I guess those are some of the qualities of comforter-friends. It's not that they are impervious to the truth. They simply know that when you've fallen for one reason or another, you don't need a sermon about what you've done wrong. They sense it's time to hone in on what your need is *right now.* What can they do to ease the situation, share the pain, assure you that they're alongside to do whatever will meet your felt need, including offering a strong arm when the leg is weak?

When you have a comforter-friend like that—who won't, as they say, kick you when you're down—you're much more prone to say rather quickly, "I wish I'd listened to you when you wanted to buy those boots. I wouldn't be messing up our walk now if I'd taken your advice." Do you suppose a lot of us would be more willing to repent, to use a biblical word, of our shortcomings and failures if we knew there was someone around who wouldn't exploit us in our moment of weakness?

When Luke the physician wrote of the life of Jesus, he told how Jesus set the direction of his earthly ministry by a reading from Isaiah at the synagogue in Nazareth (Luke 4:16-19). If I break out the verbs of that reading from all the other words, I hear Jesus saying he came to comfort, rescue, release, and heal. All the verbs of a comforter-friend. This, Jesus made clear, was the good news. Later, he gave this job description to those who followed him as well. Christ's dream seems to be that succeeding generations would do this task in an even greater and larger scope than he did.

I never saw the comforter-friend role more clearly than the time Jesus predicted Simon Peter's denial on the night of the Crucifixion. He warned Peter that he was going to fail just as Gordon had warned me that I was not prepared for the mountain walk with old slippery shoes. But while he warned

MAKING PAIN YOUR ALLY

him, Jesus didn't prevent his disciple from falling. That, it seems to me, is important. While he may not have wanted it to happen, *he let the man fail.*

But the words that the Scriptures tell us came from Jesus next were "Do not let your hearts be troubled."[1] I believe there is no coincidence in this word placement in the order of Scripture. For Jesus was looking beyond the failure to the possibilities that came afterward. He was already looking toward the time of restoration when the lessons learned from the failure would be sorted out and welded into Peter's soul. Jesus, the Comforter-Friend, thought long term—before, during, and after the fall. Most of us do not.

One wonders how often Peter, in the years that followed, looked back at that night when Jesus warned him of trouble and assured him that he was praying for him. It must have been a great lesson for Peter as to how much Jesus cared.

Not all of us are capable of being such a comforter-friend. Who of us is there that wouldn't want to be known as such? But the fact seems to be that many of us don't know how to comfort. Or we are afraid that if we set out to comfort, we are going to learn things about ourselves and life in general that are too frightening.

I'm taken with a story Stanley Jones used to tell of traveling to a clinic in rural India where a serious epidemic was going on. When he arrived at the front door of the clinic, the nurse in charge came to greet him. But when he reached out his hand to take hers, she drew her hands back.

"Don't touch me," she said. "My hands are full of the plague."

Jones never forgot those words; he repeated them often. And I haven't forgotten them either. To comfort people is to accept the risk of getting the plague of another's sadness or pain on our hearts. Occasionally, some of us are simply scared to have that happen.

One day I asked a friend who had been in a serious skiing

accident if the people who had come to visit had been able to comfort her. She admitted to me that a few had, but many had not. Most came, she said, trying to ignore the fact that she was in intense pain and that this accident would seriously inconvenience her young family for months to come.

Some had nothing to offer except to tell her to cheer up and to be assured that everything would work out. Some simply told stories comparing their own or someone else's skiing accidents. And it was not unusual for some to laugh their way through the conversation as if an injury caused by skiing were something of a comedy occurrence.

This woman was not seeking pity. She was simply telling me that many find it difficult to confront pain and discomfort in another's life. They don't know what to say because they feel they must have an answer for every question, a light for every darkness, a direction for every confusion. They want to give a quick fix, and, unable to provide it, they are frustrated and end up doing next to nothing.

Another friend once described to me the added anguish she and her husband faced when one of their children was divorced. They had the feeling when the news got out that their friends began to shun them. For weeks they felt cut off and alone. Hadn't they tried to be friends to countless people in the past when they had gone through such moments? What was being said by this isolation?

Because they are mature believers, they tried to give their friends the benefit of the doubt. Could it be, they reasoned, that people were not rejecting them but simply didn't have answers for them or know what to say?

There came a time, after the immediate pain had subsided, that they took some initiative and asked certain friends why they were avoiding them. They discovered, to their relief, that their suspicions were correct. People admitted they didn't realize that even a short prayer, a touch, or a hug when they met these friends in the church halls would have helped a great deal. A simple reminder that they weren't alone or disliked would have been a helpful gift. What the sufferer, in such encounters, needs to hear is that he or she is loved and surrounded by understanding.

A few who were in touch with themselves enough to be honest admitted that something else was happening inside of them that made them reluctant to come near. They were afraid the same thing could happen to them, and the fear of thinking about it kept them from identifying with their friends in pain. It was almost as if some suspected that a person's struggles can be infectious, and if anyone gets too close, there is a chance of the germs spreading.

A comforter-friend is different. He comes alongside and offers himself as a companion in the pain or distress. Not a sermon. Not a cliché. Not an analysis. Not even an I-told-you-so. Just himself.

We first discovered the role of the comforter-friend many years ago when our daughter Kris, then two years old, accidently drank some turpentine and was rushed to the hospital gasping for air. Gordon and I had never felt so helpless. Being a pastor, Gordon had enjoyed unlimited access to the intensive care unit. But suddenly he was barred at the door, and both of us were restricted to five-minute visits every two hours. Inside that room we knew Kris was battling for her life. The doctors told us it would be twenty-four hours before they knew the outcome. Death, brain damage, kidney failure, or a process toward healing were all possibilities.

Though that memory is twenty years old, both of us vividly recall the men and women who, as comforter-friends, came and sat with us. A prayer, an embrace, a cup of coffee, silence when necessary. They simply sat with us, sharing our pain. No answers or explanations were offered because there were none to give. As I said, they simply were present to us.

God sent Ezekiel to a colony of Jewish exiles along the Cebar River in Babylon. "I went in bitterness and anger,"

Ezekiel recalled, "but the hand of the Lord was strong upon me. And *I sat among them, overwhelmed, for seven days*" (emphasis mine).[2] As Ezekiel sat with them, he was forced to feel what they felt, and his entire attitude was modified.

When Job's friends came to comfort him in his multiafflicted state, they were precisely what he seemed to need—for seven days. They were present to him. Alongside. Silent. But when they began to experiment with opinions about Job's pain—the horror of his suffering, the reasons such misfortunes may have occurred, and their opinions about his appearance—they became more of a nuisance than a comfort.

Finally, in a moment of utter frustration, feeling totally isolated, Job shouted at them, "Look at me!"[3] or "Feel my pain. I'm a person just like you!"

One wants to tell Job that the reason he got this strange kind of treatment from his friends—hardly called comfort—was that he and his circumstances made the men feel insecure. How could they be sure that what he was experiencing wouldn't happen to them? Perhaps they were not as concerned about comforting Job as they were in comforting themselves and making sure that their own views of reality were not upset.

What could a man fear more in those days—and in our time—than the loss of his financial security, his family, his reputation? As I've suggested, it's almost as if his friends had to keep a distance of rationality or religious doctrine between themselves and Job's pain because the experience might have been catching—like that plague. If they got too close, their theology and their faith might have been rocked by a situation that had no easy explanation. So because of their own fears, they ended up debating the origins and meanings of Job's problems rather than identifying with him as a person.

God, they said, wouldn't permit these things to happen to someone who was faithful and integral (like them?). There! That settled the matter. "Now Job," they seemed to say, "admit to us what you've done wrong (so we don't have to worry about this happening to us?)."

This was a nice, neatly wrapped package—all these pat answers and explanations. But it was false security. The friends learned almost nothing, and Job suffered on without comfort. Isn't it possible that they were disillusioned because God seemed to be acting out of character—not like they thought he should—so rather than face their disillusionment, they blamed Job? It's comforting to find someone to blame.

I can't help but muse upon the "comforters" of Job and realize they wanted to explain Job's suffering in terms of a set of preconceived notions they brought to the situation. Instead of going deep with Job, asking him how he felt, what he thought all of this meant, and what he was going to do about it, they put him into theological boxes that assumed they understood his behavior and his inner attitudes. This was no comfort; this was discomfort. And yet, I see myself in their actions. Too many times I have tried to ease my own uneasiness rather than quietly enter into another's grief and pain.

If Gordon had been a "Job's comforter," he would have stood there on the pathway when I'd fallen and was hurt and said, "You were a phoney when you told me you could make this trip. You didn't listen to me when I told you your shoes were inadequate. You're obviously not up to making this trip. You can just sit there while I go on up to the top by myself. I don't walk and climb with people who fall."

But, of course, he didn't say those things. And I got up again, and we pressed on.

People's needs, the way they express them, and the way they seek to be comforted differ. I feel safe enough with my husband to tell him when I'm hurt just as I did on the pathway that day. I'm the kind who would like a few friends to walk *through* my darkness with me. But it's important to me that they not pity me or tell me only what I want to hear but are firm enough to challenge me not to avoid pain and encourage me not to quit.

Furthermore, I like to be in touch with someone who has gone through a version of my pain and can give me a hint or two of what I can expect and some of the preferable ways to face it. I like those who can help me think my way through what my pain means.

But I know others who prefer to keep their pain only to themselves. In their anguish, they would like to be left alone. When you know such a person, you can only assure him that you're available and will check in from time to time, sending notes of encouragement that need not require a response. I suppose that all of us range in between these two extremes.

I'm impressed that when Jesus was headed for the awful moment of the cross, he made no move to generate sympathy from the disciples. But he did want them close by. He asked them to "Watch with me," and "Pray with me." It was a strengthening he desired, not an easing of the pain or an escape from the suffering. Here is one of the major roles of the comforter-friend: He/she seeks to fuse strength and stamina into us, not anesthetize. The comforter-friend points to the One who will provide the "much more" that human beings cannot provide.

I will long remember a particular day that ranked as one of the lowest in my adult life. It was as if there would be no tomorrow; all the promises and the things I'd learned and taught seemed to slip away when I needed them most. I was unable to help myself climb out of a mood; a sense of despair and pessimism engulfed me. In that moment, the Lord commissioned a comforter-friend.

This was a friend, a Presbyterian pastor, who had frequently called Gordon and me. He would often send books and articles through the mail that he thought might encourage and instruct us. When we had prayer needs, we had learned that he could be counted on for intercession, often specifically checking back until the need was met.

One night he was awakened soon after he had fallen asleep. The Spirit impressed upon him the need to intercede for Gail MacDonald. In obedience, he arose and did so, on and off all night. As he read promises in Scripture, he read them with me in mind, and then he wrote them down and sent them to me the next day. Most of them had to do with hope.

This pastor had no way of knowing that I was fighting one of the great spiritual battles of my life that very night. And I had no way of knowing that he was praying. But the one thing I did know was that when I awakened the next day, the battle was over. I wrote in my journal that the suffocating heaviness of the day before seemed to have been lifted, and I described how I had new hope. The difference between the two days was as extreme as I have ever experienced. But why had this liberation happened?

Three days later our friend's letter with its written scriptural promises arrived, and then I understood why I had gained liberation from such oppression. As I read in the letter of God's nudge to this man to rise from his bed that night and pray for me many hundreds of miles away, I came to understand in a new way the role of a comforter-friend. In response to God's prompting, this man had given me a rare gift.

In my journal I wrote:

> *L. has been a pastor not unlike the angels to us. He was awakened on July 30 to pray for me. Couldn't get back to sleep, he said. Prayed Scriptures for me. And the next morning (July 31) the Lord was doing a healing work in me that has remained. The veil was lifted; hope returned; oppression ceased. And what was L. praying? Scriptures such as Eph. 1:16-19: that I would have my "heart eyes" enlightened to know the Hope to which I was called. I'll never forget this. For me, it is a charismatic experience. For a man of his stature to be touched by heaven in this way for me is heartening.*

Centuries ago, the Older Testament David had such a friend in Jonathan. Jonathan always gave David hope, value, and truth when they were together. He didn't take away the problems his father, Saul, was causing, although he sometimes tried to relieve the pressure. But he did seek to strengthen David by pointing him to God's capacity to see him through his long climb (see 1 Sam. 23:16-18).

Sometimes, as in the case of Jonathan and David, the comforter-friend can do little more than listen and allow the pain and pressure to do its work in a person's life. We can't solve other people's problems. The comforter-friend, in these cases, may have to stand to one side and simply make sure the one who is hurt is getting the right messages in the pain.

Robert Raines tells of a young woman, the wife of an army officer, who found herself living in the midst of a western desert while her husband carried on military duties. Hating desert life, she wrote a letter to her father complaining about the heat, the absence of vegetation, and the general misery of desert life. He wrote back a simple old piece of poetry:

> *Two men looked out from prison bars;*
> *The one saw mud; the other saw stars.*

Thinking through the implications of such a simple couplet, she determined to make her desert prison a place to see the stars. She began to study desert life and went on to be one of the foremost experts on desert cacti.

Her father could have made things easier for his daughter by telling her she had every right to complain. He could have sent her a ticket and told her to come home. For all I know, he could have sent her an air conditioner (if they were available in those days). But he didn't. Strangely enough, his comfort was in words of challenge. And she responded to it.

As we saw earlier with Simon Peter, the Lord did not spare his disciples the experience of struggle either. But he was always sensitive to what sort of comfort he might bring them in the midst of their stress. In the hours before and after the Crucifixion, you see him doing interesting things on their behalf that, at the time, they could hardly have appreciated.

Jesus prepared the way for these men by going *before* them at important moments in their lives together. He saw to it that the Upper Room was arranged in order that they might enjoy strength-giving fellowship. After they had failed, he made sure they received the message that he would go *ahead* of them and meet them in Galilee. This message was especially to be delivered word-of-mouth to Peter because he would need comfort more than anyone. Later, after another night of failure, the Lord was kind enough to prepare a breakfast for a group of tired and chilly fishermen/disciples *before* they reached the shore. And he has gone *before* us all to prepare a home in heaven.

Could one of the reasons we find being a comforter-friend so difficult today be the time and forethought it requires— time and forethought we are unable or unwilling to give?

Nathaniel Hawthorne worked in a government job from which he was abruptly fired one day in 1849. He came home in despair. His wife listened to his pain, then suggested he sit at a table. She brought him a pen and some ink, lit a fire, put her arms around him, and said, "Now you will be able to write the novel you've always dreamed of writing."

American literature was soon enriched with *The Scarlet Letter.* Here was the comforter-friend again. Preparing the way, giving what was needed, setting the mood. Momentary failure was turned into significant productivity.

As we take our seats at the outdoor table at the Berghaus Heimeli, I am impressed with the innkeeper's welcome. He can see by the dirt on my pants that I've taken some kind of fall. And I suspect he can tell by our faces that we're a bit tired and need this rest badly.

For a few minutes he talks with us. He listens to our account of the walk so far and tells us things about the countryside we wouldn't have known otherwise. He fills our cups a second time and begins to tell us where we will go next and what it will be like. A warning or two about difficult places. An encouragement about how much worth there will be in the effort. And finally, he speaks of what we'll see when we get to the top. He raises our curiosity and our desire to press on.

This innkeeper at the Berghaus Heimeli is the kind of person you want to meet on the climb when things get tough. He's a comforter-friend, I think as I sip my coffee; most of us need one of them rather frequently. People like this man make it possible for us to keep climbing.

MAKING PAIN YOUR ALLY

FIVE

Facing Realities

Oh God of earth and altar

Bow down and hear our cry

Our earthly rulers falter

Our people drift and die.

The walls of gold entomb us

The swords of scorn divide

Take not thy thunder from us

But take away our pride.

G. K. CHESTERTON (1874–1936)

CHAPTER THIRTEEN
The Discipline of Disillusionment

Touring Switzerland was part of a dream Gordon and I had shared for many years. But there had always been other priorities—the raising of children, writing and speaking commitments, a congregational ministry; so a journey to that part of the world had been postponed.

Then one day Gordon showed me a three-page article in the *New York Times* that described trekking in Switzerland. A woman and her husband had written in great detail about walking tours, and they described well-marked foot paths, quaint mountain *gasthauses*, and awesome scenery.

"Let's go there in September," Gordon said. This was June.

"But there's so little time to really plan the trip," I said, speaking out of my usual instinct to want to have everything in order beforehand—where we would stay each night, where we'd eat, what places we'd see each day.

"This time there will be no plan," he responded. "When we get through customs, we'll decide where to go from there.

This article gives us enough general ideas about what to do. Just this once let's do something crazy; let's go and explore."

I put the article from the *Times* to one side and then read it carefully later on to see what had caught Gordon's attention. It was convincing. Everything sounded perfect. The way the authors described things, it seemed as if one could walk effortlessly through the Alps, meeting friendly people on every hand, eating Swiss cuisine that sounded marvelous, and discovering quaint mountain hostels around every turn. Before I finished reading the article the second time, I too was a convert.

But now, a few months later, as the "walk" up the Strela became more and more difficult, I thought of that article in the *New York Times*. Like so many enthusiastically written things, it had described ideal conditions, what they call "best-case scenarios." It obviously left out what some might refer to as the downsides—the worst cases.

It did not tell me, for example, that it rains quite often in the Alps and that the rain can be chilly and uncomfortable. It didn't talk about the fact that unstable weather can settle in, causing the mountains to disappear in clouds for a week. It hadn't said that most of the great-tasting food is found in high-priced restaurants and expensive hotels. And, more pertinent to the moment, it had neglected to mention anything about some paths—like the one we were on—that seem to go straight up, testing every muscle in one's body.

Even a trip to Switzerland has its downsides, I thought. And then I recalled something that Oswald Chambers had said about downsides when it came to the larger issues of life. He was persistent in talking about what he called *the discipline of disillusionment:* the necessity of seeing things and people as they truly are—not as we would like them to be.

Disillusionment (*dis*, meaning "to be stripped of"; *illusion*, meaning "false impression" or "misconception"), as Chambers used the word, means to divest yourself of pretense—

about yourself, about others, and actually, even about God. Chambers was impatient with the idea of living in a dream-world of unrealistic and inaccurate expectations, and he liked to challenge believers to pursue the truth at all costs. So using the word in a different way than we normally employ it, he called for dis-illusioned Christians—men and women who are not surprised when the worst things happen, when evil abounds, or when the best things happen because God has unleashed his power and grace.

> *Disillusionment means that there are no more false judgments in life. . . . Many of the cruel things in life spring from the fact that we suffer from illusions. We are not true to one another as facts; we are true only to our ideas of one another. Everything is either delightful and fine, or mean and dastardly, according to our idea.*[1]

And so Chambers called us to a living of the facts, not a living of the fantasies.

There on the wanderweg to the Strela, as I felt increasingly tired and hurting, I guess I was fighting disappointment with fantasy. I'd started off from Langwies that morning anticipating little more than a long stroll. My expectations were built on the upbeat, nothing-can-go-wrong perspective of the newspaper writers. And then, as a result, I was surprised because I was engaged in a walk that was harder, steeper, and more dangerous than anything they'd described or I could have imagined. Me, naive? Of course. I should have realized that everything can't be as easy or idyllic as someone selling a product (in this case, travel) would like for me to believe it is. I should have been prepared for the facts, and I wasn't.

So it's that same sort of naiveté that Chambers was talking about when he called for the Christian to discipline himself to disillusionment. Perhaps he spoke so forcefully about this because he himself struggled with it, this tendency almost all of us have to cultivate unrealistic expectations or illusions about ourselves, about others, and even about God. His answer? Disillusion yourself!

I've learned in all sorts of ways that how we fantasize or "factualize" about people, about things, and about even God is a major issue for healthy living. If we overestimate something, we're likely to be strongly disappointed when we discover that it can't produce according to our expectations. If we underestimate something, we're likely to misuse it or squander opportunities to reap proper benefits from it.

My mind jumps to a time a few years ago when I decided to get rid of a set of four inexpensive kitchen chairs. We had originally bought them at an unfinished furniture store sale, stained them, and felt free to give them a thorough beating in our kitchen where the family ate most of its meals.

Now I felt they were no longer useful. They showed all the marks of wear and tear. Joints were loose so that they behaved almost like rocking chairs, scratches abounded, and they had a generally shabby appearance. My evaluation of the chairs was that they were beyond repair, so I put them out to be picked up by the sanitation people. But I guess I underestimated the chairs.

I happened to be looking out our front window a while later when I saw a pickup come to a screeching halt by the chairs on the curb. The driver got out and began to study them closely. He must have liked what he saw because he loaded each of them into his truck and drove off.

I found myself silently cheering the scavenger on. I was drawn to the man's spirit. My assumption that the chairs were worthless, simply because they were rickety and marred, was clearly inadequate. This man had no such illusion. He saw potential. Although the flaws were obvious, he saw them through the eye of a fix-it man; he could see what might happen if the joints were reglued, the scratches filled, and the chairs repainted. What I had discarded as valueless, another had appropriated as restorable.

As he drove off with the chairs in his truck, I found myself wanting them back. Why couldn't I reglue the joints, fill the scratches, and repaint the chairs? But then, why hadn't I seen that before? The man had "disillusioned" my view of the chairs. By stopping and inspecting them and then taking them away, he had caused me to see them in a whole new, factual light. The potential I'd not seen before I certainly saw now. But it was too late.

People who choose to follow the Lord will experience frequent disappointments of great magnitude if they do not develop this discipline of disillusionment. Unfortunately, many of us in the Christian community live by certain "illusions" or expectations. Too many of us simply have not done our homework to understand the facts about who we are as human beings and our potential for good and evil. Moreover, we have illusions concerning God as well, and when our knowledge of who God is and how he works is insufficient, it is not uncommon to fall into deep disappointment when he doesn't perform quite as we, in our ignorance, anticipated. Oswald Chambers appreciated this subtle trap, and he begged his listeners to live factually. And that meant to constantly work at disillusionment.

William Backus and Marie Chapian, in their excellent book *Telling Yourself the Truth*, put it another way. They say most of us cultivate what they call "misbeliefs," false trusts and confidences in life that are both positive and negative. Their book presses the reader to face up to unreal expectations or unnecessarily pessimistic perspectives. Their answer for this problem? They urge us to rid ourselves of such misbeliefs *by naming them, by admitting their hold over us, and by searching more deeply to find authentic belief.*[2]

Apparently, we develop this tendency to hang on to illusions about one another, about ourselves, and about God from the earliest days of our childhood. Roger Gould, psychologist and author of *The Course of Life*, points out that from infancy people live with powerfully inaccurate assumptions that are based on the illusion that human beings live in a "state of absolute safety."[3] In other words, the illusion suggests, nothing can or will ever go wrong. Gould's view of inaccurate assumptions sounds very similar to Backus's and Chapian's concept of misbeliefs.

Among the inaccurate assumptions or illusions that Gould highlights are two that I find very interesting.

One is stated like this:

> *Life is simple, not complicated. There are no significant unknown inner forces within me; there are no multiple coexisting contradictory realities present in my life.*[4]

Gould suggests that this fantasy, when cultivated, is often painfully exploded when a person reaches mid-life and becomes bewildered by the array of complexities that suddenly begin to appear in every part of life. Perhaps this is why Gordon and I have discovered that the older we get, the harder it is to make decisions and to determine the purpose of God for our lives. Life is far more complex than we'd ever realized it to be in the earlier days. The earlier view was based on a dangerous illusion; the later view, our mid-life one, can be dangerous if it leads to an inability to make decisions. Gould presents another illusion or misbelief that he thinks ambushes the naive mid-life adult: "There is no evil in me or death in the world; the demonic has been expelled."[5]

Any of us who have met evil and stared it straight in the face know that this is perhaps the most dangerous illusion of all. A failure to respect the depth of evil both within us and beyond us can eventuate in utter devastation of life. If we have a shallow view of sin similar to Gould's statement, we badly need the discipline of disillusionment.

Frankly, any effort to break free of misbeliefs is most likely to happen in the wake of a major disappointment or failure when we discover that our inaccurate assumptions have been inadequate to the test of a serious crisis. For some, the exposure of misbeliefs results in a stunting cynicism, and that is not what I'm talking about. The better alternative occurs when a person, in those hours of great pressure, examines thoroughly what is true and what is worthy of honest belief so that he might become more grounded than ever.

Earlier, I noted three areas where misbelief or false assumption can be seen most frequently. They are important to me because I have had to name them and renounce their hold over my life. I'm talking about misbeliefs about myself, about God, and about others. I'll begin with the most difficult of the three to write about. Myself.

I want to be as candid as I know how. It was not easy at all—in fact, it was traumatic—to discover that I had spent a lot of years becoming comfortable with a major illusion or misbelief about myself. Let me put it in the form of a silly proposition.

ILLUSION ONE
I'm not really capable of a major sin; actually, I've come a long way in this business of being good. God must be pleased (and not a little fortunate) to have me on his side.

Doesn't this illusion sound a bit absurd when it's written in black and white? It's a statement that is uncomfortably close to the false assumption that I quoted from the work of Roger Gould.

The painful fact I have had to face about myself is that while I have easily affirmed the orthodox Christian doctrine concerning the depravity of human beings, I have harbored inaccurate assumptions about its reality in me. And when that happens, one is reluctant to deal with either the potential or the reality of evil within.

That means there is often a reluctance to live in habitual

repentance. But, in fact, spiritually healthy adults need the self-awareness of a child who is quick to admit wrong and not ashamed to do so. For a child, understanding that things can easily go wrong inside the heart and acknowledging it is a part of life.

I'll never forget the Sunday morning when the preschool choir sang in the worship service. There must have been fifty children standing up in front of hundreds of people. Immediately after the final note of the song ended, a little cherub raised her hand and shouted, "I made a mistake, Mrs. Manganello." The congregation, as you might imagine, roared.

But here was a child who wanted to get something fixed with her teacher right away so she would not have to carry the memory of the error around with her. The power of her vulnerability, while amusing, made a strong impression upon all of us sitting there that day. *Lord,* I prayed, *make me transparent like that child.*

In *Search for Serenity,* Gigi Tchvidjian writes of the time her two-year-old son came running toward her but fell before he reached her. Getting up, he brushed himself off and said, "Oops, I dropped myself!" All of us drop ourselves—and often. But we find it harder and harder to admit to our self-inflicted hurts as we get older. We fear that if God were to hear our confession, he might be heavy-handed, as a father or some other significant person in our lives used to be.

Hiding from ourselves and others can begin very early in life. If allowed, we can become quite good at it even during our preschool years. How well I remember the five-year-old who was hurt but didn't want anyone to know it. She said, "I'm *not* crying. My eyes are just sweating!" Unlike the child in the choir, this young lady was learning how to deceive herself and others.

God had to work hard to "dynamite" from me the illusion that nothing could go wrong. I guess most of my life I have possessed what a loving friend once labelled "good flesh."

He didn't mean it as a putdown, but he knew I had tried hard to live honorably and to be as dependable, useful, and acceptable as possible.

Being a "good flesh" person is not all bad, I suppose. I knew it was only by God's grace that I was able to do anything right. But deep down, I suspect, a subtle, nagging, and very ugly spiritual pride had also grown alongside the good deeds and the calm spirit. Frankly, it was too subtle a thing for me to notice. That absurd proposition I have called "illusion one" was all the time worming its way into my inner attitude.

Fénelon was right when he said:

> The most eminent graces turn to deadly poison if we rest
> on them in self-complacent security. This was the sin of the
> fallen angels; as soon as they looked on their exalted state
> as their own assured possession they became enemies of God
> and were driven forth from His kingdom.[6]

All of this came to a head for me one terrible night in my forty-ninth year of life. It's hard for me to understand what triggered it, but an accumulation of negative feelings suddenly reached explosive potential within me. I found myself ready to lash out at whomever or whatever stood in my path. If it had not been so late at night with everyone asleep, perhaps I would have given vent to things that would have hurt those I love. So as it was, I had no one to face but myself and God as I fought the most violent spiritual battle I have ever faced.

In those lonely hours, which I shall never forget, I was forced to take a hard look at myself; all illusions and pretense were stripped away. This was not a time to study anyone else; it was rather a time to look exclusively at Gail, with her false assumptions and misbeliefs.

While others might be marked as sinners with ease because their actions are measurable and public, I began to see there resided in me a deposit of evil that was just as great as that in the meanest person who has ever lived. Perhaps my inner evil was covered with this thing called "good flesh." But my life, I came to see, no matter how good in appearance, would not stand up for a minute before God in a judgment day any more than the most obvious sinner of our time. I came to appreciate the words of St. Paul, who may have had a similar experience when he cried out: "What a wretched man I am! Who will rescue me from this body of death?"[7]

That night I learned how ugly spiritual pride is to God. And I trembled when I recalled that Jesus saved his hottest anger and his harshest words for the religiously proud. Was I one of them? If so, I was going to renounce all illusions about what was beneath "good flesh" and make my fresh pilgrimage to the cross along with the most repentant of visible sinners.

Oswald Chambers again:

> *"Be afflicted"—have you ever been afflicted before God at the state of your inner life? There is no strand of self-pity left, but a heartbreaking affliction of amazement to find you are the kind of person you are. "Humble yourself." It is a humbling business to knock at God's door—you have to knock with the crucified thief. "To him that knocketh, it shall be opened."[8]*

I see now that in the days before this cathartic realization, I often had a tendency to make quiet judgments about others because I had unconsciously carried this false illusion about myself. When others failed or sinned, was there not a tiny part of the "good flesh" in me that cried out, "How could they do that?" or "I could never be guilty of that sort of thing!"

The words of Luke burned in me: "To some who were confident of their own righteousness and looked down on everybody else, Jesus told this parable. . . ."[9] Could I be one of those? If so, Jesus had a story for me.

210

> *"Two men went up to the temple to pray, one a Pharisee and the other a tax collector. The Pharisee stood up and prayed about himself, 'God, I thank you that I am not like other men. . . .'"*[10]

The pharisee's was a "good flesh" prayer. But the Lord clearly had no use for this man's concept of prayer.

The other man, who was a tax collector and thus considered by good people to be among the worst of the worst of the worst, simply prayed: "God, have mercy on me, a sinner."[11] And for this spirit, he received the Lord's commendation. When was the last time I had honestly prayed the latter prayer?

"Good flesh" behavior may be attractive to many in the community of faith, but it can become putrid in the eyes of God if it is based on self-justification. Comparing ourselves to any standard but the perfection of Christ will always put us in a scary place. There is no other valid measuring rod. All others will lead us astray, confuse, and disappoint.

Thomas à Kempis wrote:

> *It will not hurt you at all to consider yourself less righteous then others, but it will be disastrous for you to consider yourself better than even one person.*[12]

But we have a kind God! He quickly enters the repentant heart of anyone who honestly comes to grips with the truth about self and does not cover it up. And in the wake of painful conviction comes a new awareness of the unconditional love of the one on the cross.

I remember coming to the end of the utter anguish of those hours and feeling free—washed, humbled, more clear-sighted about my real self than I'd been for a long time.

I gained a new appreciation for some of the ramifications of the story of the prodigal son that Jesus had told on another occasion (Luke 15:11-31). What newly fascinated me was the performance of the famous elder brother, whose welcome to the prodigal hardly matched that of his father.

Suddenly I began to see the elder brother as a kind of prisoner, as captive to his self-righteousness as his younger brother had been to the debauched life-style of the far-off country. The elder brother was, in fact, lost in his father's home! He was busy working *for* his father but was totally out of sympathy with his father's heart. As a result, he was unable to place true value on his younger brother. The elder brother's blindness to his pride—his "good flesh"—expressed itself in self-righteousness.

No wonder the elder brother was so miserable when he heard the shouts of laughter at the welcome-home party given for his repentant sibling. Self-righteous people may deny it, but they really don't like repentance or its resulting forgiveness and restoration. It crowds territory they feel they own.

I was startled when I recently heard someone ask the question, "What would have happened if the prodigal son, on his way back home, had met the elder brother first instead of the father?" Horrors!

If I have ever been an "elder brother," I am ashamed. I have tried to learn the importance of regularly renouncing the illusion of superiority while gratefully taking my place alongside the younger brother who said, "I have sinned . . . I am not worthy."

The bottom line of Jesus' story suggests that both sons had actually drifted from the center, the place of their father's love. For the younger, the drift had been dramatic and hostile; for the other, the drift had been subtle, covered with "good flesh." For us, the drift can also be either way.

How short the distance between being broken before God and becoming self-righteous! What once was a state of brokenness over being proud can easily drift into a state of pride over not being proud.

I am greatly comforted by the gentleness of the father with even the elder brother. He did not condemn his son for his "good flesh" attitude; he simply tried to draw him to a higher perspective while affirming his love and devotion for him. What the father desired was the love and fellowship of both sons.

No matter which captivity we choose, that of the prodigal or that of the elder brother, both are deadly. Either way the enemy of our souls is pleased.

But he is defeated when the illumination of the heart overcomes the crippling illusions of the heart. Then a person is broken. Empty of all conscious pretense or excuse.

That night, not long ago, I became a broken woman in every sense of the word. I looked beyond the "good flesh" and saw what I'd not looked quite far enough to see before— the almost infinite depth of evil that resides in me, that resides in all of us. And I was compelled to confess it with great sorrow. As I said before, it was a washing experience I shall never forget. There have been and will continue to be subsequent washings, for "self-righteousness" is not a malady from which one is cured. Rather, it requires a simple day-by-day recovery.

My spirit resonates with that of the prophet Micah when he said:

> *Where is another God like you, who pardons the sins of the survivors among his people? You cannot stay angry with your people, for you love to be merciful. Once again you will have compassion on us. You will tread our sins beneath your feet; you will throw them into the depths of the ocean.*[13]

So God punctures my illusion and shows me my need and his patience, but he also sends me out into the real world to love in the same way that he has loved me. He sends me not only to the lovable but also to those who may be less than kind, less than gracious. And in that real world the test of his life in me comes again and again: *Will I love as I have been loved?*

CHAPTER FOURTEEN
The Discipline of Disillusionment, Part 2

If you come to Switzerland with the expectation that every day will be sunny and warm, every pathway level, and every mountain easily climbed, you are in for a disappointment. Switzerland is almost everything the tourist publications say it is. But there are more than a few challenges if you want to walk the Alps: steep climbs, chilly winds, and embarrassing falls.

The walk to the Strela Pass was stripping me of all my faulty illusions about Switzerland. If I was to reach the top, and by now I was determined to do so, I would have to accept the pain and fatigue that was accumulating and keep climbing. None of the romance and beauty portrayed in the picture calendars would help me now. Being a realist about hard work, I knew it was grit and determination that would get me to the top.

Inadequate assumptions, faulty illusions. I'd had them about Switzerland, and I had them about a lot of things in life. We all have them, and they reveal themselves most distressingly in moments of personal crisis like the one I was facing on the way to the top. Our illusions about life get tested in places like that. And any flaws in our thinking are made quite clear.

If, in a moment of supreme insight, we learn some rather uncomplimentary things about ourselves, as I described in the last chapter, we also may learn some rather poignant things about our heavenly Father. We may be challenged to ask the question: Do I have right views about God? Not only about *who* he is but about *how* he does things?

Centuries ago two disciples in crisis faced that sort of question as they walked together on a road that led from Jerusalem to Emmaus. Jesus had been crucified, his body placed in a tomb. As far as the followers could see, all their expectations about a new order to life were ended with his death. They were so down that they never recognized that the third person who joined them on the journey was the resurrected Christ himself. The tomb was empty!

"What are you discussing together as you walk along?" the stranger asked them. They responded with a comment or two about the events surrounding the Crucifixion back in Jerusalem.

"*We had hoped* that he was the one who was going to redeem Israel," [1] they concluded, and in so doing, they revealed their sense of total confusion about the death of the Lord. "And what is more, it is the third day. . . ." It was their way of saying that everything had ended in dismal failure. Jesus simply hadn't operated according to the script dictated by their tastes and expectations. So they were crushed.

The disciples spoke of a hope that was past tense. But note that Jesus did not rebuke them. He simply took them back to the basics again: the Scriptures.

These followers were disillusioned by the way God had permitted things to happen. They never believed something

FACING REALITIES

like a crucifixion was possible. The cross simply didn't match their assumptions. Now, as a result, they had lost heart.

Even the faithful women, who often believed the most strongly, were disheartened. They had come earlier that day to the grave site to do what they could for a dead body. They saw no future beyond a respectable burial.

Their performance and those of the others are matched by many modern performances. Not a few of us have shared their confusion when things have gone wrong for us, too. And that's why I define a second, dangerous illusion, this one about our view of God. Put in writing, it looks as absurd as the first one did.

ILLUSION TWO
If I know God well enough, believe the promises in Scripture strongly enough, and pray with faith enough, I can be sure of what God will and will not do.

Think carefully about what I have written in the above statement. It is a cluster of words that looks good on the surface. But the kind of confidence it suggests can be quite dangerous.

There is a danger in our naive conceptions about God's work among us. We suffer from it often. We think that if we do everything right (as if we could), believe everything as perfectly as we can, and do our best to avoid all major wrongdoing, God will act predictably.

But when we hold to this illusion and something goes awry, the stability of our faith is liable to undergo a serious attack. We become unstable in our ability to trust, and wonder what else may go wrong.

Gordon and I have both gone through such crises in our personal experiences. Some years ago, Gordon had good reason to believe that God was about to make something unique happen in Gordon's world that he'd not asked for or felt he deserved. Every one of the standard indications that Christians tend to use to discern the purposes of God seemed to indicate a certain direction to events. But the conclusion of the matter did not match the earlier sense of direction.

I've listened to my husband reflect upon this moment in his life. He has spoken of the deep disappointment that followed. The disappointment was not so much that something advantageous for him did not happen but rather that he had so totally misread heaven's signals. We're all familiar with that sort of confusion. The best of us experience it.

The result of that disappointment was a brief period of disruption in his sense of intimacy with God. Not God's fault, Gordon would say; his own. Did he in fact know how to hear God speak? Looking back on it now, he reflects to me that he had put God in a box and expected one kind of answer when God obviously intended another. It was Gordon's struggle with a faulty illusion.

For me, there came a time when God answered a resounding no to a prayer I had prayed incessantly and (as far as I could see) fervently. Hadn't it been in keeping with the promises of Scripture? Hadn't elder believers concurred? Didn't the inner witness of the Spirit agree? Wouldn't it bring God honor?

It took a long time for me to be able to admit to the deep confusion I felt as a result of God's answer. Again, it was confusion over misread signals that troubled me, not that I had expected a life free from pain. It was easy to assume that God had let me down or, more bluntly, that God had failed me. But I, too, was guilty of putting God in a box and expecting him to act in a way I thought best. So neither of us is a stranger to this business of nurturing inadequate assumptions about God.

Was not John the baptizer struggling with this very same

issue when, from Herod's dungeon, he sent a message to Jesus: "Are you really the one we are waiting for, or shall we keep on looking?"[2]

What was behind that question? Doubt of a type. Jesus simply was not acting in a way or at a speed that met John's expectations or illusions. Like the men on the road to Emmaus, and like Gordon and I, he was saying, "I had hoped . . ."

But John's doubts surfaced in a safe place because Jesus did not rebuke him. Rather, he sent back what must of have been one of the most courage-giving answers. Since John's disciples had seen Jesus healing people, Jesus said:

> *"Go back to John and tell him about the miracles you've seen me do—the blind people I've healed, and the lame people now walking without help, and the cured lepers, and the deaf who hear, and the dead raised to life; and tell him about my preaching the Good News to the poor. Then give him this message, 'Blessed are those who don't doubt me.' "[3]*

What had Jesus done? He had sent John a message from the Older Testament Book of Isaiah, a volume from which they had both drawn much inspiration. In it Isaiah had spoken of the acts of Messiah, and what Jesus said was virtually a direct quotation from Isaiah 35. I'm positive that John, hearing the passage quoted and fulfilled, would have gained great strength to dissipate his doubt.

But Jesus also knew what the Isaiah passage said one verse before the passage he quoted to the messengers. John must have received courage and no little thrill as he tied the two together in his heart. For the earlier verse reads:

> *With this news bring cheer to all discouraged ones. Encourage those who are afraid. Tell them, "Be strong, fear not, for your God is coming to destroy your enemies. He is coming to save you."[4]*

This is how Jesus handled a doubting John. He could have used the moment after the messengers left for a sermon at John's expense. Would he not have been justified in saying to the onlooking crowd who had witnessed this entire interchange, "It's a shame about John. I know he's in a tough place, but he's a good example to all of us about what happens when a man doubts. Don't be like him."

Rather, Jesus' words to the crowd are: "Of all men ever born, none shines more brightly than John the Baptist."[5] At John's lowest moment of doubt, Jesus made a strong comment about his value. Jesus could handle John's doubts. They neither surprised him nor upset him.

Such doubt was never a part of my earlier life. I suppose there are some who would have labeled me not only a "good flesh" person but also an "easy believer" about most things pertaining to Christian faith. Being well-loved as a child, I had never had problems trusting in anyone in authority over me. Being able to freely trust God was included in that gift.

I identified with the story Elisabeth Elliot has told about her grandson's first visit to a drive-in car wash. She noted that he kept looking at his father whenever fear would arise in him as the monstrous nozzles squirted water all over the car and huge brushes began to scrub it. As long as his father showed no fearful reaction to all of this noise and motion, the child could relax, Elliot noted. I understood that kind of trust. It was a part of my natural inclination.

However, just as John learned more about himself in the dark moments of a dungeon, I, too, had to admit one day not long ago that I was trapped in this second illusion. Unconsciously, I had come to the conclusion that I knew what God would and would not do. But there came a day when he allowed the absolute opposite of all my expectations to happen.

For a long time afterward, I could not even admit to myself that I was struggling with a colossal case of doubt. Scripture reading was difficult; praying by myself was a battle. There were hard questions deep down within that I was afraid to recognize and ask.

Perhaps I was in a similar state to Teresa of Avila when someone pushed her cart into a gutter. She got up, looked heavenward, and with a smile said to God, "If this is how you treat your friends, no wonder you have so few."

It was hard for me to admit to doubt. Never having struggled with it, I was reluctant to face it when it came. In fact, I'd often had a rough time when anyone close to me admitted to doubt. I found it hard to understand what bothered him. But now it was bothering me.

I actually needed a friend to suggest the possibility of doubt to me. It was our conversation that liberated me to face the fact that I was indeed a doubter. My friend did much for me that day, including teaching me the meaning of the biblical adage, "Faithful are the wounds of a friend."[6]

When we feel as if we are swimming in a sea of disappointment and confusion, we often need to find another person who will spend a significant amount of time with us to help us gain perspective. And frankly, in this busy world, that is almost impossible. But God gave me a friend who pointed to the source of my struggle and the illusion that was causing it. Now that I think of it, Jesus was being the same kind of friend to the two who walked to Emmaus.

Once I was able to acknowledge my doubt and raise the issue to God, as John had done to Jesus, I could get on with the process of "disillusioning" myself about concepts I had had no right to hold God to.

To understand this disillusionment, I turned to those who were . . . well, disciplined—men and women of the past who had learned, sometimes the hard way, to say yes to the unexpected and unexplained in their lives. Our favorite phrase for studying these kinds of people is "listening to the deep" because that which comes from the pen of a suffering person has infinitely greater depth than that from the pen of one who has known only success.

Eric Liddell understood what it meant to face all sorts of mystifying circumstances that at first made no sense. He had learned there could be no person-made boxes for his God.

It is said Eric Liddell had the most awkward running style of any athlete of his time. Ian Charleson, the actor who played Liddell's character in the film *Chariots of Fire,* said it was difficult to emulate his running style because he ran with his head back. When Charleson attempted it, he kept running off the track or bumping into other runners.

By the sixth day of filming, Charleson said he finally understood what Eric Liddell must have been doing. He recalled that in drama school he and others had engaged in what they called trust exercises. They ran as hard as they could toward a wall, trusting someone to stop them. "I suddenly realized—Liddell must have run like that. He must have run with his head up and literally trusted to get there. He ran with faith. He didn't even look where he was going."[7]

Liddell had stepped away from a great athletic career and the promise of a celebrity's life-style in England to become a missionary in China. Once there, he ended up in a Japanese concentration camp where he died at a relatively young age from a brain tumor.

But Eric Liddell lived and died as he ran. With his head up. Trusting. His favorite words were "Absolute surrender" and "Be still, my soul." His final words to his friends were simply "It's complete surrender."[8]

I am quite sure that Liddell would not have chosen to die in a prison camp at a young age. His children were not yet raised, and because of the war, he was away from his family. But he died peacefully, nevertheless. Why? Because he had learned not to ask God questions that arose out of preconceived illusions. Peace came through absolute surrender to the sovereign ways of God.

Fénelon could have been Liddell's mentor in this matter of

surrender. He wrote: "If there is anything that is capable of setting the soul in a large place, it is absolute abandonment to God."[9]

I went on consulting the writers of the deep. Oswald Chambers was next in line.

> *There is only one thing God wants of us, and that is our unconditional surrender. . . . [Have] simple perfect trust in God, such trust that we no longer want God's blessings, but only want Himself. Have we come to the place where God can withdraw His blessings and it does not affect our trust in Him?*[10]

Did Oswald Chambers go through some devastating experience in life that made him write so insightfully? Gordon and I have read through his thoughts from one end to the other. Can anyone write with such depth if he has not been to that depth himself? One wonders.

> *Someday we shall understand that God has a reason for every no which He speaks through the slow movement of life. How often, when his people are worrying and perplexing themselves about their prayers not being answered, is God answering them in a far richer way.*[11]

Those were the words of Lettie Cowman, author of such devotionals as *Streams in the Desert*, who knew all sorts of challenges to the common ideals or illusions a woman might have. Her husband, Charles, had left a secure job in American railroading to become a missionary in Japan. He took her to what was then a very difficult place to live with no promise of financial support. For the rest of his life, she watched him invest the entirety of his energies in the establishment of what became the Overseas Missionary Society and die at a relatively early age from utter exhaustion.

Amy Carmichael, another voice from the deep, wrote:

O thou beloved child of My desire,
Whether I lead thee through green valleys
By still waters
Or through fire,
Or lay thee down in silence under snow,
Through any weather, and whatever
Cloud may gather
Wind may blow—
Wilt thou love Me?
Trust Me?
Praise Me?[12]

Or consider the words of Etty Hillesum two short months before she would die in the gas chambers of Auschwitz. Though not yet a prisoner herself, each day she voluntarily worked in the prison camps, helping people cope with what was ahead. Engulfed in loss and death, she wrote:

I now realize, God, how much you have given me. So much that was beautiful and so much that was hard to bear. Yet whenever I showed myself ready to bear it, the hard was directly transformed into the beautiful. . . . To think that one small human heart can experience so much, O God, so much suffering and so much love, I am so grateful to you, God, for having chosen my heart in these times, to experience all the things it has experienced.[13]

These men and women were rare and treasured gifts to me. They had also faced illusions and expectations and dissipated them. They had agreed to let God be God. Their words were "seam binders" (Remember that term?) to me, and their affirmations reminded me that God did indeed care about the smallest details of this discontinuity in my spiritual journey.

Yes, I concluded, God could do with me whatever he chose.

FACING REALITIES

I would cease trying to write his script. The lack of my earlier trust had to be confessed and renounced. I would be willing to live by *every word* that came from God, not just the ones I could understand.

We are in great danger of losing our hearts during times of testing. If our walk with Christ is short-lived or immature, we may lose confidence in God or slip into the awful captivity of anger and bitterness. Such possibilities should not be taken lightly. For me, the testing time became a period of deepening as I readjusted my understanding of God's ways. But, sadly, others whom I have known have turned away from faith completely under similar circumstances. I believe Thomas à Kempis was correct when he said, "Two things increase temptation's hold on you—an indecisive mind and little confidence in God."[14]

I have come to embrace the truth behind the following story. Charles Spurgeon once traveled to the countryside to visit a friend who was building a new barn. On the roof was a weather vane with the text "God is love." Spurgeon asked if the man meant God is as changeable as the weather.

"No!" the man exclaimed. "I mean it to say that God is love no matter which way the wind blows."

During the ministry years of Jesus, a Canaanite woman came to him and asked him to heal her daughter. At first, Jesus, seeming to be less than compassionate, made no response. In fact, his disciples suggested that he send her away because she was becoming a nuisance. When the Lord did speak to her, he further tested her resilience by saying he was restricting his ministry to the people of Israel.

Still she persisted—and not angrily or impatiently, as far as we can see. She simply came, knelt, and pled again. Her faith was so unshakable that Jesus finally affirmed her and healed her daughter. For me, the important part of that story is that she returned to kneel and worship him *anyway* even though it seemed at the time that her concerns were rejected.

Someone has noted that our ability to believe God seems to have three phases. In the first, least mature phase, we need something like a sign or powerful feelings to stabilize us. In the second phase, we may no longer need signs or feelings, only favorable circumstances that point toward an ultimate answer to our questions. But the third and most mature phase is reached when our trust in the Lord is independent of circumstances, emotions, human reason, or even the opinions of others. We simply learn to trust.

You see that third sort of maturity in men like Moses and David, who heard a lot of yesses but also heard some large noes. Moses, for example, was told he would die before reaching the Promised Land, something he'd looked forward to for forty years. But his faith was not dashed or injured. His was the mature reaction: "I'll train Joshua."

It had been King David's hope to build Jerusalem's first temple. But the Lord said no and told him his son Solomon would do the job instead. David's reaction? He would put all of his labor and resources into the preparation that would make things as easy as possible for Solomon. Again, that's maturity.

Fortunately, there are models for that kind of trust in God in modern times as well. Two people who have inspired us are Christy and Betty Wilson, who served Christ and his people in Afghanistan for years. As a pastor in the city of Kabul, Christy Wilson led his congregation in the building of a fine church sanctuary. There came a time when the Wilsons were forced by the Islamic government to leave the country. They had no desire to leave, but circumstances beyond their control seemed to prevail; so their ministry in Kabul ended. Later, another command came to the church from the government: Abandon the new building because it will be destroyed.

Gordon and I remember receiving a telegram from interested Christians that called on followers of the Lord throughout the world to pray for the protection of the church building. Hundreds of thousands of believers prayed with faith. We implored the Lord individually and corporately to spare this one place of public Christian worship in Kabul. Then we waited for a miracle of deliverance. A miracle that never came, at least as we defined a miracle.

One day bulldozers belonging to the Afghan military arrived to destroy the church property. The Wilsons were now in the United States. Betty told us later of Christy's reaction when they learned that the building had been reduced to rubble. He simply fell to his knees and gave thanks. Why the giving of thanks? Christy Wilson reasoned that his congregation was learning how to say yes to anything God permitted.

And learn they did. The believers at Kabul had met the soldiers and their heavy equipment at the church site and served them tea and cookies while they undertook their mission of destruction. No wonder Dr. Wilson gave thanks.

I am impressed that the Wilsons and the Afghan Christians did not whine or cry "foul" when God did not choose to answer their prayers to save the building. Theirs was a faith built on no false illusion. They believed that God was love no matter which way the wind blew. Their concern was to obey God and even to love their enemies. Serving them— even refreshing them—was more important than crying in protest when something special of theirs was taken away. Their behavior was a miracle, I think—a miracle according to God's script, not ours.

When we believe that God is in control no matter what the circumstances, all sorts of inner stability enters life. Nien Cheng has recently written of her six years of virtual solitary confinement by the Red Guards in China. Stripped of almost everything of importance, including her only daughter, who experienced a tortuous death, she was placed in a cell. One day she found her attention fixed on a small spider that began to spin an intricate web near the window. The spider was something Nien Cheng would never have noticed in a more normal setting. But on that day, when there were no distractions, she watched it with intensity.

After the spider was finished, she pondered what she had just seen and what it meant.

> *I had just watched an architectural feat by an extremely skilled artist, and my mind was full of questions. Who had taught the spider how to make a web? Could it really have acquired the skill through evolution, or did God create the spider and endow it with the ability to make a web so that it could catch food and perpetuate its species? How big was the brain of such a tiny creature? Did it act simply by instinct, or had it somehow learned to store the knowledge of web making? Perhaps one day I would ask an entomologist. For the moment, I knew I had just witnessed something that was extraordinarily beautiful and uplifting. Whether God had made the spider or not, I thanked Him for what I had just seen. A miracle of life had been shown to me. It helped me to see that God was in control.*[15]

Here is the secret, as Nien Cheng found it in her own seam-binding moment: When you affirm that God is indeed in control, you no longer have to pin your life to artificial and sometimes inaccurate conceptions of who God is and what he may or may not do.

This is a much harder affirmation than any of us imagine, and one needs to be careful before issuing a glib positive response. For it is not unusual for us to experience many noes on the way to an ultimate yes.

Two centuries ago, an Englishman, William Carey, culti-vated an ambition to be an agricultural laborer. He loved gardening. But a skin ailment kept him from working in the fields, and he was finally forced to learn a new trade: shoemaking and repair.

The man who trained Carey in his new skill just "happened" to be a godly man who knew Greek. As the two men worked together, Carey not only learned the shoemaking trade, he also learned Greek from the Greek New Testament. In the process, Carey began to receive a vision for world evangelization. It was a case of an *initial no* leading to God's *ultimate yes,* for William Carey became the father of the modern Protestant missionary effort.

The death of Betsy ten Boom in a Nazi prison was a brutal *no* to Corrie, her sister. But it was the pathway to God's ultimate *yes*: the fleshing-out of a forgiving heart for which Corrie ten Boom became known around the world.

When Joni Eareckson Tada was horribly injured in a dive into shallow water, it was a glaring *no* to normal life. But God's ultimate *yes* has been seen in her remarkable, growing ministry to the disabled of our world. She has literally awakened the consciousness of the evangelical church to a ministry never before taken seriously.

John Perkins heard the initial *no* when his brother was killed in a Southern racial incident years ago. But he heard God's ultimate *yes* years later when God called him back to Mississippi and the formation of the Voice of Calvary Ministries, which has been such a precedent-setting work among blacks.

A friend of mine, Linda, a New England pastor's wife, was washing her clothes in the basement of her home when a man entered the cellar door and, without a word, began to stab her until she fell virtually lifeless to the floor. Her husband, Rich, was at a church meeting, and when he returned home, he found Linda alive but unconscious. For days, her life hung in the balance.

To this day, the assailant has never been identified. But Linda has survived and has returned to health. When people have said to her, "God was so good to have spared you," Linda replies, "God is good whether I had lived or died."

That has been God's ultimate *yes* to Linda. Her faith gained strength because of God's felt presence throughout her ordeal. Her faith has never been stronger.

And then there is another friend I have never known except in the books she has authored and whom I have quoted throughout this book of mine, Amy Carmichael. When the past twenty years of her life were spent in bed because of a serious accident, she cautioned people against playing "if-only" games as they recalled the night of the injury. In fact, her injury could have been much worse in that the ambulance that drove her to the hospital nearly had a fatal crash.

> *If [the ambulance] had gone over, would we say prayer was unanswered? It is a petty view of our Father's love and wisdom which demands or expects an answer according to our demand, apart from his wisdom.* We see hardly one inch of the narrow lane of time. *To our God eternity lies open as a meadow. It must seem strange to the heavenly family who have seen the beautiful end of the Lord, that we should ever question what love allows to be, or ever call a prayer unanswered when the answer isn't what we expected. Isn't no an answer? And when a "fatal" accident occurs, I feel like adding, "Isn't heaven an answer?"*[16]

God's ultimate *yes* for Amy had to do with the books she wrote from her bed; they are her deepest and most insightful, ministering to millions.

The list goes on and on of people who learned that God was in control and discovered that was all they needed to know. No illusions were necessary.

When we are tied to the initial noes rather than the ultimate yes, it is usually because we have put conditions upon God as I did. Our misbeliefs, our illusions, our preconditions are all constraints we try to place on our Father. They must go.

The pastor of the New Hampshire church where we attend when we are at Peace Ledge once told the story of two little French girls, Denise and Maria. Denise fell into a pond one day while the two were playing, and Maria managed to grab her long hair and hold her head above the water until help came. The press picked up the story of Maria's heroic gesture and came to interview her. How, they asked, had the incident changed her life? Her answer: "Denise won't play with me anymore; she says I pulled her hair."

So it would seem that sometimes God pulls our hair when, in fact, he may be saving our lives. This can only be appreciated by an inner spirit that is free from the illusions that chain God to our expectations.

When we cast aside our illusions about God and exchange them for truth about who he really is, we must understand that life may change for us. Our goals can never be prosperity, ease, convenience, or the lack of pain. We can only hope to mean it when we say with Amy Carmichael: "My goal is God himself . . . at any cost, by any road."

He who shall pass judgment on us
is the one who made us in frailty.
ROBERT LOUIS STEVENSON

CHAPTER FIFTEEN
The Discipline of Disillusionment, Part 3

One of my favorite entertainers is humorist and musician Victor Borge. On one occasion, when Borge was performing in Flint, Michigan, the crowd was very sparse. Undaunted, Borge looked out at the slim audience and said, "Flint must be an extremely wealthy town: I see that each of you bought two or three seats."

Some entertainers would have been upset by a plethora of empty seats; they might even have canceled the event. Not Borge! He seems to have known how to handle those moments when people let him down, and he was prepared to give his best to those who hadn't. You can say that he had "disillusioned" himself in terms of his expectations of people's performance. He knew how to act in the midst of disappointment. That's something we all need to learn.

It is easy to cultivate a strange hybrid of expectations about others. We actually live under the faulty assumption that no one, at least those whom we love and to whom we have given much, *should* or *will* ever disappoint us. This assumption is a nice idea, but that is all it is—an idea or an ideal. It does not conform to reality. It never has. Everyone, sooner or later, *will* disappoint us.

The important issue is whether or not we will be prepared to handle that moment when it comes. Because if we are not, a world of people only too ready to let us down will sooner or later leave us in a state of bitterness and paralysis.

When people fail or disappoint us and we are unprepared for it, the normal human response is to feel rejected. Distance grows between the offender and the offended, which probably means the relationship will never again be the same. When we are hurt, we often express a prolonged sense of shock and dismay, as if we thought this sort of thing could never happen. And in so doing, we reveal something strange about all of us. We give evidence to an illusion or fantasy in our view of humanity that could be put in another of my strange-sounding, even silly, statements.

ILLUSION THREE
Believing that sin is a serious defect only in people who are plainly evil, we base our friendships and associations on the assumption that by nature we are good and will never fail one another.

It is hard to convince most confessing Christians that this is a common illusion because our theology affirms the depravity of humanity. However, what we say theologically about humanity's sinfulness and how we respond when someone acts out that theology can be two totally different things. In other words, we affirm the existence of sin but may not quite know what to do with the sinner.

Jesus knew what to do. He was never surprised or ambushed by evil in human beings. Speaking of the origins of
sinful behavior, he said:

> "Out of the heart come evil thoughts, murder, adultery,
> sexual immorality, theft, false testimony, slander. These are
> what make a man 'unclean'. . . ."[1]

John provided an interesting insight into Jesus' view of
people when he wrote, "Jesus would not entrust himself to
them, for he knew all men."[2] It's a way of saying that while
the Lord loved people deeply, he was not unaware of their
potential for the worst kind of behavior or betrayal.

But this is not to say that he didn't have an equally high
view of people to offset what might be called a low view of
their potential for evil. No one provides a better model for
how to love people and raise them to greater levels of living
quality than Jesus. His ability to see what people could become—good or evil—was astonishing. Over and over again,
he reached out to men and women whom most of us would
have dismissed as useless, and through his love built into
them the highest values and the most powerful performances
in the kingdom of God.

Nevertheless, one never sees cynicism or vindictiveness in
Jesus when these same men and women momentarily fail.
Such bad moments would shatter most of us because we so
badly want to believe an illusion of progress that suggests
that good people will never make a bad choice.

At a critical time in my life-climb, when I might have been
devastated had I believed this third illusion, a friend gave me
an essay by Parker Palmer, a Quaker educator, that greatly
helped and challenged my understanding. In it, Palmer asks
this insightful question: On the evening of the Last Supper,
*why was the Lord willing to stay at the table when he knew that
the men about him would be such miserable failures by the end of*

the night? Somehow that question has managed to drill itself deeply into my soul, and it has caused me to look at people in a totally different way.[3]

Would we have stayed at a table with people whose major preoccupation during the evening seemed to be only themselves—their own personal interests and positions of importance in the group? Would we have stayed at the table with those who seemed to lack the slightest sense of self-awareness—who, despite all their protestations of faithfulness and courage, would run at the first sign of danger a few hours later? Wouldn't most of us have gotten up from the table that included people like that and left in disgust? I think I might have. Unless, that is, we had come face to face with similar weaknesses within ourselves.

In the strictest sense, it wasn't that Jesus saw the same potential in himself. Rather, he simply knew this potential was in everyone. Because of this, when he saw the great disparity in his disciples' empty words and what he knew to be their upcoming performance, he was not moved to leave. He had a *factual*, not an illusory, view of who these men really were. But at the same time, he had a gracious love for them. The result? He stayed at the table. No illusions. No need to be painfully distressed in the hours ahead when they let him down.

To repeat: Nothing surprised Jesus. Even though his disciples were clearly headed into failure, he gave them every chance ahead of time to avoid it and every grace afterwards when they were living with the consequences.

Would that Jesus could have enjoyed the experience of having his disciples worship him that night as the Lord he really was. Would that he could have been refreshed with their expressions of thanksgiving and the assurance that they had heard what he taught them. Unfortunately, what he had to endure that night was their pettiness, their competitiveness, and their empty promises.

If the centerpoint of their relationships was their own perceived goodness and adequacy, it was, as Parker stated, a romantic idea, an illusory view of community that would dissipate at the first spectacular failure in the garden.

But if, on the other hand, his Lordship and Grace were the centerpoint of their communion, they would be free to be truthful with one another at the table about their fears and potential failures. And later, in the aftermath of defeat, in those dark moments of embarrassment, they could have found mutual strength to rebound as they recovered. Fortunately, following the Crucifixion, they did come together and helped each other rebuild.

Wherever community is based on human goodness, a subtle fear spreads. We become increasingly anxious about owning up to the evil in our hearts because we know we fall short of the perceived standard that has been defined as goodness. It becomes easier to affirm the doctrinal definition of sin and depravity but harder to repent when that sin is actually present. It becomes possible to point the finger at other sinners but difficult to admit that we ourselves have personal struggles.

Why? Because the fellowship is based on maintaining a legally described level of goodness, and one becomes fearful of losing the fellowship and acceptance that comes when everyone thinks you're adhering to the rules. The prospect of being rejected by a group we love and admire makes vulnerability and transparency about our fears and failures highly unlikely.

Because this matter of illusion is so prevalent among modern Christians, it is not unusual to find many who are reminiscent of the king of Samaria, who once wore hidden sackcloth under his kingly purple robe (2 Kings 6:30). Apparently, he wanted to perpetuate the illusion on the surface that all was well in his kingly life. But underneath the illusion of wellness, there was sackcloth, the symbol of deep personal anguish and distress. He was scared, brokenhearted, and ashamed. But no one was going to know about it if he could control the information.

All of this suggests we ought to be most careful when we include the word *grace* in our theological and institutional identifications unless we are prepared to grant it when one of us turns out to be exactly what our Christian theology says we are: struggling, recovering sinners who are prone to failure at any moment.

When Gordon and I had been married only a couple of years, we experienced a deep disappointment. A friend whom we knew and loved was caught embezzling some money.

Today, more than twenty years later, I reflect back on my reaction to this friend and this sin with much sadness. My reflection centers on my regrettable role—or lack of role—rather than on what she did. I gave little grace. Instead of helping my friend face the facts of her sin, discover the causes of it deep within herself, and pick up the pieces and go on, I guess I simply became preoccupied with my own disappointment and spent valuable time licking my own wounds. How immature I was. It was a hard lesson for me, and it was learned at someone else's expense.

I have often wondered if my friend tried to signal me that she was in trouble but could not bring herself to share the full truth until it was too late because she feared my rejection. And that thought causes me to wonder if any friendship is genuine if either party in the relationship fears such rejection from the other. Is a friendship really a friendship at all if the relationship dissolves when one fails the other?

There is no way I can justify the sin of embezzlement, of course. Jesus never treated the sinful actions of anyone glibly. But neither did he break communion with any man or woman who was genuinely contrite in the wake of sin. His perspective always seems to have been built on the long-range view. It was as if he said on each occasion, "I'm not surprised by what has happened; I grieve over the consequences you'll face; but noting your broken and sorrowful spirit about this thing, I anticipate great things from you when you've learned from these wrong choices."

As with friendships, the community of faith ceases to be a community if there is no freedom for us to approach the cross together and individually acknowledge that we are by nature not good, that evil thoughts and sometimes evil deeds mark us. There must be a place for us to tear open our robes and reveal the sackcloth, not fearing rejection or relegation to second-class citizenship. There must be a place to find hope and strength to try again.

As I replay the process of my failure to be a friend years ago to one guilty of embezzlement, I wonder what might have happened if I'd been more of a person with whom my friend could have felt transparent. Did she sense that I would have rejected her had she told me of her temptation to siphon money from her boss's accounts? And would I have rejected her if she had told me that this was what she was thinking about?

I wish I could be sure that my reponse would not have been avoidance but rather deep personal concern and a desire to help her move to the core of what was causing her to feel tempted. I wish I could be sure that I would have loved her enough to hold her accountable to right behavior. I wish I could be sure that, if she had told me of her temptation, I would have made her feel safe enough in my Christian love to deal with this dark place in her inner being and prohibit it from ever eventuating in an evil deed. For early, honest repentance is the key to not carrying out our temptations or repeating our actions if we have succumbed.

But none of that happened! For whatever reason, she did not open her heart to me about the temptations or, later, the actions with which she was living. If she had felt free to take that first step, I suspect that life for her would be different today. This is a difficult memory for me.

It may be that part of the reason we end up being so devastated by the failures of others is that we tend to brand people, label them, nicely categorize them in neat packages. It is not a new observation to say that Western Christians are often prone to use labels. People are theologically right or wrong, spiritually carnal or spirit-filled, in or out of the faith.

But anthropologists and students of Middle Eastern culture tell us that Jesus did not see people in terms of boxes and labels. His invitation was not to join an organization or sign a statement but rather to "Follow me." Simply, "Follow me." It was a directional and relational matter, not an organizational, doctrinal, or positional one. He was concerned about men and women moving in the direction he was moving; he was concerned that they receive grace for what they knew themselves to be. He would take it from there.

Again, this is no license for us to go on being as we once were. It assumes that one who is genuinely following Christ will steadily draw closer, rising higher than the former evil life-style, repudiating the sin that is within and without. But there will be momentary setbacks and reversals in this process. Jesus knew that and accepted it. We must do the same.

The disciples had a hard time learning that relationships were based upon direction rather than position. Following Jesus' transfiguration before Peter, James, and John, the Twelve asked Christ about a man who was outside the organization, as they saw things.

"Master, we saw someone using your name to cast out demons. And we told him not to. After all, he isn't in our group." But Jesus pointed them away from the membership or positional concept and toward the directional idea: "You shouldn't have done that! For anyone who is not against you is for you."[4] In other words, if they're not going away from you, they must be traveling with you.

It wasn't long after this that the disciples expressed bitter indignation toward the people of a Samaritan village who refused them and the Lord a night's hospitality. "Master, shall we order fire down from heaven to burn them up?"[5] Interestingly enough, the question seems to have been asked by John, who would later write, "Dear friends, let us practice loving each other, for love comes from God."[6]

The John who wished to destroy a village and the John who encouraged people to love at all costs are the same man simply several decades apart in personal development. If the Lord had rejected the young, immature John who had hatred in his heart, then we would never have heard from the older, apostolic John who later shows us a better way. Having received correction and grace in the midst of his poor performance, he was ready to urge us on to grace in ours. Being a recipient of grace, he became a champion of it. Having been given a second chance, he urged us to give second chances.

The elder John understood the importance of asking which direction a person is headed rather than thinking in terms of hard, fixed categories of belief or position. It assumes that the life of faith is a process of becoming rather than one of near-perfection.

In the previous chapter, I quoted words from the diary of Etty Hillesum, who died in Auschwitz during World War II. Frankly, as I initially read her words, I found myself uncomfortable. Much of her behavior in the earlier phases of her life was repugnant to me, and I was tempted to resist the value of her story because I couldn't get past the first part.

But I'm glad I gave Etty Hillesum space to learn and grow because her spiritual awareness became increasingly plain as time passed and she allowed pain to open her heart. As she applied to her life what she read in the Scriptures, she became transformed from a woman who could have become steeped in anger and hatred to one greatly aware of the nearness of God. I was rebuked by her increasing wisdom and depth.

I came to see her steady movement, directionally, toward Christ.

> *On Thursday evening, the war raged once again outside my window and I lay there watching it all from my bed. . . . Yet I felt so deeply peaceful and grateful, there in my bed, and meekly resigned to all the disasters and pains that might be in store for me. All disasters stem from us. Why is there a war? Perhaps because now and then I might be inclined to snap at my neighbor. Because I and my neighbor and everyone else do not have enough love. Yet we could fight war and all its excrescences by releasing, each day, the love which is shackled inside us, and giving it a chance to live. And I believe that I will never be able to hate any human being for his so-called "wickedness," that I shall only hate the evil that is within me, though hate is perhaps putting it too strongly even then. In any case, we cannot be lax enough in what we demand of others and strict enough in what we demand of ourselves.[7]*

Had not the God of all truth slowly but surely opened up Etty Hillesum's heart to his truth? By the time of her imprisonment and subsequent death at the hands of the Nazis, she was faithfully reading the Gospels and the works of St. Augustine. She came to understand the ugliness of evil and the beauty of an open, receptive heart to a loving God.

Could it be that in the last thirty years we have reacted to preaching and teaching on evil to such an extent that we have only wanted to hear how good we can become? Did we, in fact, throw the baby out with the bathwater? Have we lost our understanding of the power of evil within us and in the world about us?

Oswald Chambers:

> *It is not being reconciled to the fact of sin that produces all the disasters in life. We talk about noble human nature,*

self-sacrifice and platonic friendship—all unmitigated nonsense. Unless we recognize the fact of sin, there is something that will laugh and spit in the face of every ideal we have.

Unless we reconcile ourselves to the fact that there will come a time when the power of darkness will have its way, and that by God's permission, we will compromise with that power when its hour comes.

. . . The man who accepts salvation from Jesus Christ recognizes the fact of sin, he does not ignore it. Thereafter he will not demand too much of human beings.

. . . Jesus Christ never trusted human nature, but He was never cynical, He trusted absolutely what He could do for human nature.[8]

C. S. Lewis also spoke directly to this issue when he said, "Until a man finds evil unmistakably present in his existence, in the form of pain, he is enclosed in illusion."

Or to come at this same perspective from an entirely different source, Gordon and I recall the words of an Episcopal rector who, in his morning sermon, said, "There are no super-Christians; there are only super-receivers."

Jesus never left the Twelve, or anyone else, for that matter, in a state of rejection over failure when there was repentance. His only anger and hostility (if it's fair to perceive a hostile Christ) seemed to be aimed at those in high religious circles whose self-righteousness had made them critics of everyone else and judges over who was right with God and who had the credentials to say anything about him.

No, Jesus goes to the point of people's failure because he anticipates it and talks about what they will need next: repentance, grace, restoration, a new and better way. Keep practicing; keep climbing, he seems to say to each struggling trekker who finds the trail a lot harder and steeper than anticipated.

This magnanimous spirit was taught to the disciples after

the incident I mentioned earlier involving the inhospitable Samaritans. Not only did he rebuke John for his attitude, but a few days later, Jesus used a Samaritan to illustrate superior kindness in the story of the Good Samaritan. How easy for us to hold grudges toward those who have refused us a kindness or to expect the same behavior from them the next time. Not Jesus. No, he seemed rather to believe that next time they would get it right.

Observe his spirit even during the moments of his greatest anguish. He sadly watched his disciples sleep through three occasions when he had asked them to pray with him in the garden. When the ordeal was over, he did not say to them, "I'm through with you," but, "Arise, let's go [on to the next experience]." His patience was absolutely remarkable. He fulfilled the meaning of the Older Testament phrase, "All day long I have held out my hands to an obstinate people" (Isa. 65:2, NIV).

What do we learn from all of this? We learn that when we are disappointed by someone close to us, we have a choice: the mind of Christ or the mind of an arbitrary, opinionated, rigid judge.

The mind of Christ will draw us to pray for another's heart to become soft and repentant and to turn in a new direction. The mind of Christ will cause us to pray for the errant and hurting friend, asking that through the pain of consequence, he or she will choose to do things differently the next time. The mind of Christ in us will cause us to grieve greatly out of love and draw us to want to shower the one who has caused disappointment with restorative grace.

But the mind of the judge will demand justice and retribution and seek some sort of appropriate vengeance, whether it be embarrassment or reparation or a host of other possibilities. The mind of the judge may very likely want to use a bad situation in another's life to gain higher ground in a relationship and turn it into a position of control. The mind of the judge will take a position of smugness, knowing that when another person looks bad, the one sitting in judgment will look better by contrast.

It is a striking fact that Jesus never said a judgmental word to a repentant person. Rather, knowing what was in that person that might have caused a bad choice or the formation of an unrighteous value or a panic from fear, he simply said, "Here's my hand; let's start over."

We often bring this third illusion or false assumption about people to marriage. A woman writes to me about her disappointment in her husband:

> *My struggle is being married to a believer who does not want to take leadership for anything spiritual in our home. He's content to be spiritually fed on Sunday mornings at church or through Christian radio. But he is not interested in taking over as head of our home. It causes such disappointment and sometimes resentment that I have to read and pray alone or be the one to initiate spiritual fellowship. I thought that marrying a Christian would automatically make a Christian home. I was wrong.*

I suspect this woman has expressed the same opinion to her husband on many occasions. She has made a set of judgments, and perhaps they are technically correct. But again, they are built upon illusions, preconceptions she brought into the relationship and demands upon her husband. Rather than create a climate of patience and growth, she has permitted herself to grow negative and disappointed. Resentment toward her husband captures her spirit because he is not living up to her ideal. He no doubt feels her disappointment, receiving its signals in her words, her facial expressions, and her actions.

If we believe people won't change, they won't. Human beings have an uncanny way of locking each other into past behavior.

On the other hand, I have spent many hours in the past

couple of years in touch with women who have been deeply disappointed by a husband's marital infidelity. In almost every case, I've seen these women embrace the discipline of disillusionment and go beyond forgiveness. Having recognized their false illusion that sin is a defect that can't touch nice people, and aware that the only true fellowship of Christ's people is based on Christ's lordship, they have chosen not to absorb themselves in blame and vengeance but rather to move on to grace and restoration. They have discovered, as have I, that we are interdependent; we often help one another to sin or not to sin. And we need to accept responsibility for both possibilities.

We need not be forcibly disillusioned. If we rid ourselves of the illusion that others must not fail us, we will grow in the freedom of staying with others to the end of their climb, imperfect though they be.

In our twenty-seven years of marriage, Gordon and I have accumulated thousands of feet of movie film and thousands more photographs and slides of the great and small moments of our lives. These all commemorate moments in the past; there are more pictures to take in the future.

When our children were teenagers, they were never that eager to see pictures of their childhood because they didn't want to be identified with the embarrassments of their pasts. And I've come to appreciate that when any of us have experienced a major setback or failure, we feel much the same way. There are always those in our paths who seem to want to take us back to the past and show us old movies about our more tragic moments. As far as they are concerned, whenever they meet us, they want to take those pictures out again.

Not Christ. It's almost as if he threw out all of the old pictures and said, "Life is not a photograph upon which your existence is frozen for all of time; it is rather a movie or a video that continues on and on. And if it has had some sad moments at certain times, it can have grand moments at other times." Watch the movie, not the photograph. Note the pro-

246

cess, and remember that it is the entire climb that counts, not just the fall.

> *Search thine own heart*
> *What paineth thee*
> *In others in thyself be:*
> *All dust is frail, all flesh is weak*
> *Be thou the true man thou dost seek.*
> —John Greenleaf Whittier

The pathway up to the Strela Pass grows steeper and harder. No, the woman in the *New York Times* didn't say anything about walks like these. No one did. But as I lift one foot after another, I see we are going higher and higher to levels I didn't think possible even an hour ago, and I gain excitement and confidence about reaching the top.

There are no longer any illusions about this trip. It is a hard physical climb we are making. But something within us compels us to continue. The satisfaction of an unusual accomplishment? The increasing beauty of the scenery? Maybe there is even a healthy fear of failure, of turning back prematurely and never knowing whether or not we could have made it.

Perhaps there is also a sense that we are engaging in a parable about other things in our lives where effort is necessary and goals demand perseverance. Maybe God is using this experience on the mountain slope to plant within our spirits an important message about the future. Maybe he is saying that in life there are always going to be painful falls (although I hope not too many) and chilly winds and steep trails and that we should not cultivate illusions that it will be easy.

Maybe on this climb to the Strela Pass God is saying, "I want you to remember this day for the rest of your lives—how you didn't quit, how you kept climbing." And we remember.

Focusing
on the Goal

CHAPTER SIXTEEN
The Riveted Eye

There comes a point on the path to the Strela Pass when the walker must cross a fast-moving mountain stream. A couple of logs lie across the cold, rushing water, and if you want to get to the other side, which we did, you have to walk their length with the balance of a high-wire acrobat. To slip means soaked feet, ruined pride, and the chills.

On the other side, the pathway turns sharply upward. Soon it is almost hands-and-knees climbing. Arduous, to be sure, but not unnecessarily dangerous. The map—which we studied more closely later—warns of this stiff climb and notes that this part of the walk is "strenuous" in contrast to other parts of the walk that are only considered to be "rambles" (the map's language; not mine). My body, of course, would have rather "rambled," and it had its ways of informing me that this strenuous part of the trail was not part of the agreement I made with it when I'd awakened in Langwies earlier that morning.

In a little while, we were high above the valley floor, and the top of the pass, which had once seemed so far away, now became a visible objective. We knew we were on the homestretch. Behind us, below in the valley, was the continuous music of the cowbells and the roar of the stream we'd crossed on the log bridge.

Halfway up this last slope, which seemed to me more like an Everest-like precipice, was a tiny, grassy knoll—an inviting resting place. A pipe from a mountain spring emerged from the ground, and sparkling, cold water poured into a trough made from a hollowed-out log. Carved on its side was a German phrase—probably wishing the drinker a safe journey—and a date—probably indicating the day the trough was set in place. The trough with its artistic lettering was one more example of the kind of craftsmanship the Swiss seem to put into all of their work.

Gordon and I sat there on the grass, munching fruit, Swiss chocolate, and a pastry our Langwies friends from the Backerei Konditorei had given us earlier in the morning. The spring water was our beverage; the sky was our roof; and the magnificent Alps were our decor. This incredible mountain restaurant was a gift from God. All the tiredness from the long walk and even the pain from several falls were quickly forgotten. I guess it was one of those occasions when the clock seems to stand still, and you say to yourself, "I'm made for these moments of timelessness." This was a Sabbath in our climb, the last time we'd take a long rest before we reached the top.

Suddenly my reverie was broken when we heard the bark of a dog from the valley far below. Along the pathway where we had earlier walked came a farmer with a large dog following closely at his heels. The two were headed toward a herd of brown cows that was scattered in the grass on either side of the Alpine stream.

Our binoculars brought the scene closer. It was clear that

the farmer intended to round up his cows and move them to another pasture. He and his dog would do the job together.

We should have moved on, but we were too fascinated by what came next. The farmer simply pointed to a distant cow, and the dog instantly bounded off. As the dog approached the cow, it began a frenzied barking and nipping at its hind legs. When the cow could abide the nuisance no longer, it began moving in the direction of the farmer. That caught the attention of other cows in the area, and soon they were all on the march.

The dog returned to the farmer when his task was completed. He sat directly in front of him, tail wagging, eyes fixed, waiting for the slightest gesture that would send him off again on another assignment. The farmer stood on high ground watching the herd's movements, and finally, he pointed a second time. Immediately, the dog moved into motion, and within a few minutes another group of cows was headed in the direction the farmer wished.

With great fascination, we watched this sequence for at least a half hour. Each time, the farmer and his dog performed perfectly as a team. Nothing impressed us as much as the dog's attentiveness to the wishes of his master. We were both amazed at what appeared to be the dog's single-mindedness as it would return again and again, sit, and wait for the next command.

From our Sabbath perch high up over the valley, the two of us carried away that picture of the dog with his eyes upon his master. It symbolized the kind of devotion we have come to learn that must be given to the heavenly Master. And we prayed that afternoon for a similar "riveted eye" that waits for the Master's slightest gesture.

A writer of the psalms says:

> *I lift up my eyes to you, to you whose throne is in heaven.*
> *As the eyes of slaves look to the hand of their master, as the*

eyes of a maid look to the hand of her mistress, so our eyes
look to the Lord our God, till he shows us his mercy.[1]

As I have already noted, this was not the easy walk we had imagined when we started out that morning from Langwies. What had kept me going? Many things. The good time Gordon and I were having talking; the fun of seeing the things you'd only find in Switzerland; the inner determination to finish what I'd started. There is a spirit within all of us that presses us to keep climbing, that doesn't want to give in to the other part of us that wants everything to be easy, that opposes the contrasting spirit of mediocrity that seeks the greatest returns for the least investment.

Other motivations? There had been the encouragement Gordon and I had given one another and the promise I made to myself that a few falls and bruises were not going to get the best of me. The innkeeper at the Berghaus Heimeli had been a cheerleader; he was sure we could make it.

And now there was this dog whose eyes were focused only on his master. Even in that working partnership, I heard a message that would keep me climbing not only up the mountain to the Strela Pass but also up the slopes that mark out my life. I would rivet my eyes on my Master, Christ. I would doggedly pursue my three-point mission. And I would seek the process of becoming like him and him alone. I knew there would be many times in the future when I'd look back at this climb in the Alps and say to myself, *I kept climbing then when the stakes were small; I'll keep climbing now when the stakes are large.*

We need that sort of message, every one of us. Those among us, for example, who would like to quit a marriage that has suddenly turned sour; it may be time to get the eye riveted back on the goal of making a relationship work and keep climbing. Those among us who would like to beg out of a commitment to a task that's only half-done; we need to get our eye back on what we started to do and keep climbing.

FOCUSING ON THE GOAL

Those among us who have fallen into a terrible failure and disappointed others and ourselves; we need to remember the long-range mission that got us started, get up, and keep climbing. In each case, the eye has to be riveted toward heaven.

For a long while after we resume our climb to the top, I think about the farmer's canine assistant. It occurs to me that this is a dog that doesn't know how to complain. I know I'm stretching my analogy, but it's helpful to my thoughts. The dog down in the valley has only one thing in mind: the master's purpose, not his own convenience.

In contrast, I'm mindful of another dog Gordon and I meet each day when we take our daily walk back at Peace Ledge. It's almost a three-mile stroll when we walk around the large New Hampshire pond near our home on the hill, and halfway through the walk, we come to a house where a large black dog lives. His name is Dunno. Dunno is a stray that wandered in out of the woods one day and settled on that home for his residence.

"What's his name?" someone asked the home owner one day soon after he'd appeared.

"I dunno," came the answer.

And that's how it happened. Dunno stuck as a creative name for a dog that appeared out of nowhere.

Apart from loudly barking at every passerby, Dunno seems worthless to me. As we walk the path every day, Dunno is waiting for us. He lies lazily in the sun until we are about twenty-five yards away and then explodes into noise. He seems to want to express great hostility toward anyone who uses the path, and he usually keeps on expressing himself until we are a hundred yards farther down the road. Then he lies down again and resumes his wait for more walkers at whom he can bark.

I try to compare the Swiss farming dog to Dunno. But really, there is no comparison. The one begs his master for a chance to serve. The other begs people to bug off. The one wags his tail in a burst of enthusiasm; the other seems to gripe and complain at the slightest disturbance.

Which am I, Lord? I ask as I silently press toward the top of the pass. *Do you ever label me a barking complainer and a loafer in the same way I visualize Dunno back at the pond? How often do you see me as being like the vigorous dog who is anxious to serve down there in the valley?*

Pere Didon, well known for his work with children in the late nineteenth century, wrote to those who wanted to come and work alongside of him:

> *I do not want people who come to me under certain reservations. In battle you need soldiers who fear nothing. Enlarge yourself then, and may noble sacrifices never appear to you too burdensome. Never say to yourself, "It is enough," but keep rising higher. Feelings are of very little value; the will is everything. God will not take you to task for your feelings, for it is not within the power of man to ward them off, or allay them. That which God looks at in the human soul is the will. The only thing that lies within our power is to will, to love.*[2]

Gordon estimates that it's only a few hundred yards to the top now, and although I hear that, I feel my legs turning to jelly. We may be close to the top, but that does not stop me from wanting to resist even one more step forward. It would be very easy right now to do the complaining I have so far avoided doing, to let my partner-in-climb know that this was far too strenuous a "walk" for us (at least me) to undertake, to say what I think about our failure to have read the map more closely or to have quizzed the innkeeper back in Langwies a bit more carefully. But instead, I determine to keep headed toward the top that Gordon says is only a short distance away.

John Ruskin wrote of times like these when he said:

FOCUSING ON THE GOAL

Taking up one's cross means simply that you go on the road which you see to be the straight one; carrying whatever you find is given to you to carry as well and as stoutly as you can; without making faces *or calling people to come to look at you.* . . . *All you have to do is keep your back straight as you can and not thinking about what is upon it—above all, not to boast of what is upon it.*

The moody and complaining spirit can easily dampen the desire not only of the one who is climbing but of those who are alongside. F. B. Meyer once recalled how, as a young man, he had struggled with irritablity. An older man shared with Meyer that he had found relief from this sort of mood by looking up at the very moment he felt the anger reaching its peak and saying, "Thy sweetness, Lord."

Meyer claimed that this not only had greatly aided him but had helped the tens of thousands he shared it with. It has worked more than once for me, too, and you can be sure I was employing the Meyer secret as I kept climbing. "Thy sweetness, Lord."

It works in the hour of any sort of temptation. The temptation to deceit? Thy truth, Lord. To be impatient? Thy patience, Lord. Frenzied? Thy calmness, Lord. To strike out with a biting word? Thy kindness, Lord.

I have kept my eye on the top for so long now and have refused to listen to the pain and fatigue in my body. It's clear that if I'd known what this walk was really going to be like, I would have resisted the challenge. But all the negatives are but a memory now because suddenly, almost anticlimactically, we reach the top. We're here! We've done what I had been tempted to think might be impossible. Impossible to us, anyway—not to a host of Swiss senior citizens and small children, among others, who fairly jog to the top of places like this.

But no matter. It's us, Gordon and me—we are here. And what I've looked at for so long from a distance is now the place where I stand. Suddenly, the fatigue is forgotten; the bruises are no longer meaningful. We have kept climbing, and, as a result, the Strela Pass is ours.

FOCUSING ON THE GOAL

EPILOGUE
At the Top

Gordon and I were at the top, the place we'd climbed toward for hours. For a moment, we stood silent, our arms about each other, out of breath. We looked back down the trail, tracing the route of our ascent as far as our eyes could see. The chalets of Dorfli were visible far in the distance. And there, further up the valley, was the Berghaus Heimeli, where we had met the encouraging innkeeper. We could easily see where the trail began to follow the mountain stream for a couple of kilometers until it reached the two-logged bridge. Finally, we traced the steep pathway leading to the grassy knoll where we'd eaten our lunch beside the water trough and watched the farmer and his dog.

Again and again, we hugged one another in sheer exhilaration. We'd made this climb, we two fifty-year-olds. We'd shared the lovely vistas, the learning experiences, the difficult moments. We'd done it without a sharp word between one another. We'd participated in an event that would be important to us for the rest of our lives.

We would talk about this day over and over. We'd try to describe it to friends and show them the pictures we'd taken. But already, we knew they wouldn't understand why this could be such a meaningful experience. They weren't there. They were on their own climbs. But this one was ours—its painful moments, its magnificent ones.

The two of us were sure we wouldn't have attempted the climb to the Strela Pass if we'd known what was ahead of us. Grand naivete! How many other climbs in life would we also have avoided if we'd realized at the beginning what we knew halfway up the slope. At the onset of every climb, there is always enthusiasm and vision. At the end, there is accomplishment and pride. But between, there is usually more work, more pain, more fatigue than anyone anticipates. Nevertheless, when climbs are over, we're all mostly overjoyed that we kept climbing.

The trek to the Strela has been just a day's adventure during a vacation. But in this adventure, I've reaffirmed a principle within my heart. Repeatedly, I've seen the climb to the Strela as a picture of the dimensions of my life.

Every day, for example, is a climb of one sort or another. Each day, early in the morning, I usually sit at the table where I have my personal worship and make a list of the things I want to accomplish before the day is over. I write down the incidental and significant things I want to get done, prioritize them, estimate the cost in terms of time and energy, and make out something like a schedule. I do it even though I know there will be be important interruptions, phone calls, unanticipated problems, unexpected visitors, and mindless distractions.

And after the planning, the day's climb begins. I usually go through many of the same experiences on each daily climb that I've had on this mountain trek. Every day there are the falls, the fatigues, the surprises. And it is a rare day that ends exactly as it was outlined.

What keeps one from turning off the trail during the daily climb, even from turning back? Perhaps it begins with knowing where the top is and determining to get there one way or another.

Then there are also the stages of life that can be likened to a climb. Some of us are young adults, and our climb is in that period of life where we have to establish ourselves in a marriage, in a vocation, in the development of children. It's a climb that can be as long as five, ten, or more years. We start with the same sort of enthusiasm Gordon and I reflected when we first left Langwies: The world, the pathway, or anything else can be easily conquered in a day. We can handle anything.

Some of us are mid-lifers, and we know that the climb isn't quite the same as we thought it might be when it began. We now know what young adults can never understand: The climb is tough, exhausting, and more routine-oriented than glamorous. We know what the young do not know: You need a lot of stamina, a lot of grace, and a lot of flexibility to make it to the top.

In this long climb, there are more than enough challenges to make the journey both thrilling and exhausting. There will be frequent temptations to deviate, to leave the trail for other pathways that look more inviting and easier to walk. There will be temptations that invite a fall and distractions that invite laziness, making the top impossible to reach in daylight. There will be the tendency to avoid important rest stops and refreshment times. And there will be the question as to who is sharing the climb with us so that we have encouragement, protection, and companionship.

I have lived long enough to read something in the faces of those in the last phases of the climb, the seniors just ahead of me. I'm aware that some of them are on hands and knees crawling to the top, and I'm encouraged to see some of them standing at the top.

As I've looked ahead, I've seen the complaining face, the bitter face, the regretting face. But I've also seen the faces of those who are serene and satisfied in the knowledge that they've given the climb everything they are worth. They have been arrested by the surprise of living, a simple gratefulness to be alive. And they are reaching the top with great strength of spirit.

These climbers are not necessarily those who have the strongest bodies you've ever seen. Often they are in their seventies or eighties. But their spirits are strong, and they cannot be deterred as they head for the top.

Some of the closest friendships Gordon and I enjoy are with men and women in the seventh and eighth decades of their lives. These are climbers whose minds are as fertile and flexible as anything we have ever seen in people half a century younger than they are.

They feed their minds every day of their climb. They collect new ideas and new impressions with the enthusiasm of the gold miner who thinks he has struck a mother lode. They ask questions from everyone in order to learn. They pray with fervor and read the Bible and seek the face of God with the same eagerness they had decades before. They have mastered the secret of the riveted eye.

These climbers never complain. They seek to encourage. They are kind; they are generous; they are filled with grace. They are not startled at the failure of a younger person because they have seen all the possible falls that can victimize a climber, and they've taken a few themselves.

These older climbers speak with wisdom. Their words are economical. They know that gossip and slander are useless expenditures of valuable time. They put a premium on every hour and put their affairs in order, for they do not know what hour will be the one in which the top is reached.

I find myself wanting to be very close to climbers like these because I never leave their presence without growing and learning. I love to hear them talk, and from them I learn what is truly important. I suppose I want to be roped in (as they say of mountain climbers) with these kind of climbers because I want to be one of them myself someday.

So Gordon and I stand at the top of the Strela Pass, and we contemplate the beauty of the Alps. And then, as the wind dies down a bit, we hear something in the distance that we'd not heard until this moment. Music! Swiss music—an accordion and a horn or two. Where might it be coming from? We feel like we're at the top of the world. We haven't seen anyone since we watched the farmer and his dog.

We follow the source of the sound around the side of an outcropping of rock. Gordon is a few yards ahead of me, and so I'm surprised when he begins to laugh, because I don't see anything that is funny.

And then I, too, see what caused his laughter. For there, not more than a hundred yards away, is a huge mountain restaurant. Hundreds of people are sitting around eating and drinking in the afternoon Alpine sun while a Swiss band serenades them.

I'm shocked! We are not alone. We are not the only ones at the top of this mountain pass. Half of Switzerland seems to be here. How did they get here?

The truth is that many climbed up the other side of the pass. Some came by a tram several kilometers in length that comes up from the town of Davos. Others walked much easier trails that climb to the top from that side. Only Gordon and I seemed to have come up from the Langwies side, the more difficult trail.

As we approach the restaurant, no one seems to notice or

care that we have arrived to join them at the top. They have no sense that we have just accomplished a dramatic ascent that will be fresh in our memories for years. There are no cheers, no stirring welcome. We're just another couple of walkers, folks who, like hundreds of others, are at the top enjoying themselves.

Soon we are at a table in the Strela Pass Restaurant, opening our map and studying it more carefully than we'd done earlier. Only now do we discover that there are other ways and other trails that lead to the top. In our ignorance, we had chosen the difficult way. So that was why we'd been so alone in our climb.

I thought about the Bible characters, some of whom I've already mentioned, who thought they were the only climbers in the world. Elijah, who said, "Only I am left." Moses, who inferred that he was the only faithful one in the crowd. Peter, who seems to have thought that he was the only one Jesus could depend upon in the end. But there were always other climbers, approaching the top in different ways and different speeds.

It was not my privilege to say to everyone that my way was the only trail to the pass, and it was not mine to boast of my hardships on the way up. For as I looked out upon the crowd of us there at the top, I realized that some had probably faced a greater challenge than I had. Surely there were some who were aged or not feeling well who could have told other kinds of horror stories. And some had had an easier time of it than I had. But the important point was that we were all here. We'd kept climbing. The goal had been reached.

The Christian believes the promise of Christ. That Christ has gone to the top of the longest, highest climb first. He came from the top; he has returned to the top. There he lives today in the presence of the heavenly Father. He prays for us all, the Bible says. He prays for us in our high moments and in our lows. He is sensitive to every fall, every moment of fatigue, every temptation to quit and turn back. He offers a steadying and directing hand to all who seek him.

And best of all, the Bible makes it clear that he is ready to welcome the climber who reaches the top after him. His is the hand that beckons, dare I put it in words like these, to the "restaurant" at the top where there is joy, celebration, and praise led by a heavenly band.

The climb is a day; the climb is a period of life; the climb is a specific challenge in life. The climb is life itself. And the challenges, the obstacles and temptations, the strength-giving elements, and the joys all seem to be similar in theme and possibility. But in every case, there is one important point to remember always: To reach the top, you've got to keep climbing.

NOTES

INTRODUCTION
1. Rom. 8:29, NIV.
2. Amy Carmichael, *Gold by Moonlight* (Fort Washington, Pa.: Christian Literature Crusade, 1951), 71.

CHAPTER 1
1. Luke 19:10, NIV.

CHAPTER 2
1. John 12:1-8; Mark 14:3-9.
2. David Lyle Jeffrey, *A Burning and a Shining Light* (Grand Rapids, Mich.: Eerdmans, 1987), 252-253.
3. 1 Sam. 25:3, NIV.
4. 1 Sam. 25:32-35, NIV.
5. *New Hampshire Sunday News*, 18 September 1988.
6. Charles Whitfield, *Healing the Child Within* (Deerfield Beach, Fla.: Health Communications, 1987), 18-19.
7. Megan Marshall, *The Cost of Loving: Women and the New Fear of Intimacy* (New York: Putnam, 1984), 40-41.

CHAPTER 3
1. Esther Howard, "The Care and Feeding of IALACs," *Faith at Work* (March 1974), 23.
2. For a closer look at sensitivity and how to develop it, see *If Those Who Reach Could Touch* (Revell).

CHAPTER 4

1. Mark 14:9, NIV.
2. François Fénelon, *Spiritual Letters to Women* (Grand Rapids, Mich.: Zondervan, 1974), 203.
3. Malcolm Muggeridge, *Confessions of a Twentieth Century Pilgrim* (San Francisco: Harper and Row, 1988), 48.
4. Edward England, *An Unfading Vision* (London: Hodder and Stoughton, 1982), 53.
5. Ibid., 54.
6. Oswald Chambers, *Leagues of Light* (Louisville, Ky.: Operation Appreciation Ministries, 1984), Introduction.
7. Ibid., 19.
8. John C. Pollack, *Hudson Taylor and Maria* (Eastbourne, England: Kingsway Public, 1984), 178.

CHAPTER 5

1. 1 Tim. 1:13-14, NIV.
2. Carmichael, *Gold by Moonlight*, 80.
3. Acts 7:60, NIV.
4. Acts 9:17, NIV.
5. 2 Tim. 2:26, NIV.
6. Rom. 5:6, TLB.
7. Margaret Magdalen, *Jesus, Man of Prayer* (Downers Grove, Ill.: InterVarsity, 1987), 134.

CHAPTER 6

1. Armand M. Nicholi, Jr., *Hope* (Cambridge, Mass.: Harvard University, n.d.).
2. 2 Cor. 2:11, TLB.
3. See Matt. 18:18.
4. Luke 23:34, TLB.
5. 2 Sam. 1:19-20, 22-23, TLB.
6. Phyllis Thompson, *D. E. Hoste* (London: Lutterworth Press, 1947), 121.
7. Prov. 10:12, NIV.
8. James 2:12-13, NIV.
9. Gen. 50:21, TLB.
10. Bob Considine, "Edith Taylor's Story," *Reader's Digest* (1966), 73-75.

CHAPTER 7

1. Deut. 8:10-14, 18, TLB.
2. Thomas R. Kelly, *A Testament of Devotion* (New York: Harper, 1941), 79.
3. Anne Morrow Lindbergh, *Gift from the Sea* (New York: Random House, 1955), 57.

4. G. Campbell Morgan, *The Gospel According to Mark* (Westwood, N.J.: Revell, 1927), 151.
5. Amy Carmichael, *Learning of God* (Fort Washington, Pa.: Christian Literature Crusade, 1985), 119.
6. Mark 6:31-32, NIV.

CHAPTER 8
1. Mark 6:36, NIV.
2. Exod. 32:24, NIV.
3. Ps. 139:23-24, TLB.
4. F. W. Boreham, *Shadows on the Wall* (London: Epworth, 1922), 44.
5. Thomas Kelly, *Testament of Devotion* (New York: Harper and Row, 1941), 61.
6. Fénelon, *Spiritual Letters*, 16.

CHAPTER 9
1. Ps. 106:12-13, NIV.
2. Exod. 17:14, NIV.
3. Josh. 4:2-3, NIV.
4. Morton Kelsey, *The Other Side of Silence* (Mahwah, N.J.: Paulist Press, 1976), 199.
5. Ps. 73:1, NIV.
6. Ps. 73:21-26, TLB.
7. James D. Knowles, *Memoir of Ann H. Judson* (Boston: Gould, Kendall and Lincoln, 1849), 100.
8. Ibid., 168.
9. Ibid., 173.
10. Ibid., 174.
11. Ps. 141:8; 142:3, NIV.

CHAPTER 10
1. 1 Cor. 2:3, NIV.
2. 1 Kings 19:18, TLB.
3. Acts 18:9-10, NIV.
4. Nicholas Wolterstorff, *Lament for a Son* (Grand Rapids, Mich.: Eerdmans, 1987), 89-90.
5. John 12:27-28, TLB.
6. Amy Carmichael, *Edges of His Ways* (Fort Washington, Pa.: Christian Literature Crusade, 1955), 178.
7. Isa. 45:3, NIV.
8. Amy Carmichael, *Toward Jerusalem* (Fort Washington, Pa.: Christian Literature Crusade, 1936), 85.
9. Amy Carmichael, *Rose from Brier* (Fort Washington, Pa.: Christian Literature Crusade, 1933), 74-75.

CHAPTER 11

1. C. W. Hall, *Samuel Logan Brengle: Portrait of a Prophet* (Chicago: Salvation Army, 1933), 89.
2. Harold Begbie, *The Life of General Booth, vol. 1* (New York: Macmillan, 1920), 289.
3. James Buchan, *The Expendable Mary Slessor* (New York: Seabury, 1981), 25.
4. Frank Houghton, *Amy Carmichael of Dohnavur* (Fort Washington, Pa.: Christian Literature Crusade, 1979), 49.
5. John 3:27, NIV.
6. Corrie ten Boom, *Clippings from My Notebook* (Nashville: Thomas Nelson, 1982), 89.
7. Isa. 46:3, NIV.
8. Carmichael, *Gold by Moonlight*, 149.
9. Carmichael, *Rose from Brier*, 19-20.
10. Begbie, *General Booth, vol. 1* 302.
11. Fénelon, *Spiritual Letters*, 129.
12. Heb. 12:3, NIV.
13. Gigi Tchvidjian, *Thank You, Lord, for My Home* (Minneapolis: World Wide: 1980), 96.
14. Carmichael, *Gold by Moonlight*, 75.

CHAPTER 12

1. John 14:1, NIV.
2. Ezek. 3:14-15, TLB.
3. Job 6:28, TLB.

CHAPTER 13

1. Oswald Chambers, *My Utmost for His Highest* (New York: Dodd, Mead and Co., 1954), 212.
2. William Backus and Marie Chapian, *Telling Yourself the Truth* (Minneapolis: Bethany, 1980) 135.
3. Roger Gould as quoted by Judith Viorst, *Necessary Losses* (New York: Ballantine, 1986), 313.
4. Ibid., 314.
5. Ibid., 315.
6. Fénelon, *Spiritual Letters*, 246.
7. Rom. 7:24, NIV.
8. Chambers, *My Utmost*, 297.
9. Luke 18:9, NIV.
10. Luke 18:10-11, NIV.
11. Luke 18:13, NIV.
12. Bernard Bangley, *Growing in His Image* (Wheaton, Ill.: Shaw, 1983), 29.
13. Mic. 7:18-19, TLB.

KEEP CLIMBING

CHAPTER 14
1. Luke 24:21, NIV, emphasis mine.
2. Matt. 11:3, TLB.
3. Matt. 11:4-6, TLB.
4. Isa. 35:3-4, TLB.
5. Matt. 11:11, TLB.
6. Prov. 27:6, KJV.
7. Sally Magnusson, *The Flying Scotsman* (Boston: Charles River Books, 1982), 37.
8. Ibid., 169.
9. Fénelon, *Spiritual Letters,*
10. Chambers, *My Utmost,* 297.
11. Mrs. Charles E. Cowman, *Streams in the Desert, vol. 1* (Grand Rapids, Mich.: Zondervan, 1986), 307.
12. Carmichael, *Gold by Moonlight,* 32.
13. Etty Hillesum, *An Interrupted Life* (New York: Washington Square Press, 1981), 207.
14. Bangley, *Growing,* 36.
15. Nien Cheng, *Life and Death in Shanghai* (New York: Penguin, 1988), 143.
16. Amy Carmichael, *Rose from Brier,* 151.

CHAPTER 15
1. Matt. 15:19-20, NIV.
2. John 2:24, NIV.
3. Parker T. Palmer, "On Staying at the Table: A Spirituality of Community," *Expressions* (May-June 1986).
4. Luke 9:49-50, TLB.
5. Luke 9:54, TLB.
6. 1 John 4:7, TLB.
7. Hillesum, *An Interrupted Life,* 98-99.
8. Oswald Chambers, *A Place of Help* (Fort Washington, Pa.: Christian Literature Crusade, 1973), 190-193.

CHAPTER 16
1. Ps. 123:1-2, NIV
2. Amy Carmichael, *Whispers of His Power* (Old Tappan, N.J.: Revell, 1982), 198-199.

BIBLIOGRAPHY

BIOGRAPHY AND AUTOBIOGRAPHY

Abbott, Evelyn, and Campbell, Lewis. *Life and Letters of Benjamin Jowett.* New York: Dutton, 1897.*

Allen, Alexander V.G. *Life of Phillips Brooks.* 3 vols. New York: Dutton, 1901.*

Anderson, Courtney. *To the Golden Shore: The Life of Adoniram Judson.* Valley Forge, Pa.: Judson, 1987.

Begbie, Harold. *The Life of General Booth.* 2 vols. New York: Macmillan, 1920.*

Bentley-Taylor, David. *My Love Must Wait: The Story of Henry Martyn.* Downers Grove, Ill.: InterVarsity, 1976.

Bertrand, Louis. *Saint Augustine.* New York: Appleton and Co., 1914.*

Buchan, James. *The Expendable Mary Slessor.* New York: Seabury, 1981.*

Bunyan, John. *Grace Abounding to the Chief of Sinners.* New York: Penguin, 1987.

Chambers, Oswald. *Leagues of Light.* Diary, 1915–1917. Operation Appreciation Ministries, Inc., Louisville, KY 40206.

Cheng, Nien. *Life and Death in Shanghai.* New York: Penguin, 1988.

Choy, Leona. *Andrew Murray: Apostle of Abiding Love.* Fort Washington, Pa.: Christian Literature Crusade, 1978.

Cowman, Lettie (Mrs. Charles). *Missionary Warrior.* Robesonia, Pa.: OMF Books, 1928. Biography of Charles Cowman.

Crago, T. Howard. *The Story of F. W. Boreham.* London: Marshall, Morgan, & Scott, 1961.*

Dodds, Elisabeth. *Marriage to a Difficult Man: Jonathan and Sarah Edwards.* Philadelphia: Westminster, 1971.*

Elliot, Elisabeth. *A Chance to Die: The Life and Legacy of Amy Carmichael.* Old Tappan, N. J.: Revell, 1987.

———. *Shadow of the Almighty: The Life and Testament of Jim Elliot.* New York: Harper and Row, 1979.

Goforth, Rosalind. *Jonathan Goforth.* Minneapolis: Bethany, 1986.

Hall, C. W. *Samuel Logan Brengle: Portrait of a Prophet.* Chicago: Salvation Army, 1933.*

Hopkins, Hugh. *Charles Simeon of Cambridge.* Grand Rapids, Mich.: Eerdmans, 1977.

Houghton, Frank. *Amy Carmichael of Dohnavur.* Fort Washington, Pa.: Christian Literature Crusade, 1979.

Jeffrey, David Lyle, ed. *A Burning and a Shining Light: English Spirituality in the Age of Wesley.* Grand Rapids, Mich.: Eerdmans, 1987.

Jones, E. Stanley. *A Song of Ascents: A Spiritual Autobiography.* Nashville: Abingdon, 1979.

Kerr, Hugh T., and Mulder, John T., eds. *Conversions.* Grand Rapids, Mich.: Eerdmans, 1983.

Lean, Garth. *God's Politician: William Wilberforce's Struggle.* Colorado Springs, Colo.: Helmers Howard, 1988.

Ludwig, Charles. *Mother of an Army.* Minneapolis: Bethany, 1987. Biography of Catherine Booth.

Magnusson, Sally. *The Flying Scotsman.* Boston: Charles River Books, 1982. Biography of Eric Liddell.

Moody, W. R. *The Life of Dwight L. Moody.* 1900. Reprint. Westwood, N.J.: Barbour, 1985.

Muggeridge, Malcolm. *Something Beautiful for God.* Harper and Row, 1971. Biography of Mother Teresa.

Murray, Iain H. *Jonathan Edwards: A New Biography.* Carlisle, Pa.: Banner of Truth, 1987.

Newton, John. *Out of the Depths.* New Canaan, Conn.: Keats, 1981.

Petersen, William J. *Martin Luther Had a Wife.* Wheaton, Ill.: Tyndale, 1983.

———. *C. S. Lewis Had a Wife.* Wheaton, Ill.: Tyndale, 1985.

Pollock, John. *Hudson Taylor and Maria.* Robesonia, Pa.: OMF Books, 1967.

Roseveare, Helen. *He Gave Us a Valley.* Downers Grove, Ill.: InterVarsity, 1976.*

Sangster, Paul. *Doctor Sangster.* London: Epworth Press, 1962.*

Sargent, John. *Life and Letters of Henry Martyn.* Carlisle, Pa.: Banner of Truth, 1985.

Smith, Goldwin. *William Cowper: English Men of Letters.* 1880. Reprint. Philadelphia: Richard West, 1980.

Taylor, Geraldine. *Pastor Hsi.* London: Morgan and Scott, 1900.*

Thompson, Phyllis. *Climbing on Track.* London: C.I.M. Publications, 1954.*

———. *D. E. Hoste.* London: C.I.M. Publications, 1947.*

Trueblood, Elton. *While It Is Day.* Richmond, Ind.: Yokefellow, 1983.

Wayland, Francis. *Memoir of the Life and Labors of Adoniram Judson.* 2 vols. Phillips, Sampson, and Company, 1854.*

*These titles are out of print as far as I know. Many of them can be located at seminary libraries or rare and used bookstores. We found all of ours at used bookstores in New England.

The serious reader of biography will no doubt prefer two-volume works as opposed to single volumes that only give high spots. For instance, the Judson volumes compiled by Wayland have all of Judson's letters and journal entries, whereas the biography done by Courtney Anderson is far less detailed but well worth the reading.

Where to start? If I could find Begbie, Dodds, Hall, Hopkins, Houghton, Jones, Magnusson, Pollock, and Thompson, I would have found enough insight and stimulation to last for months.

SNATCH BOOKS (When Time Is Limited)

Baillie, John. *A Diary of Private Prayer.* New York: Scribner, 1979.

Bangley, Bernard. *Growing in His Image.* Wheaton, Ill.: Shaw, 1983. A reinterpretation of Thomas à Kempis's *Imitation of Christ.*

Carmichael, Amy. *Edges of His Ways.* Fort Washington, Pa.: Christian Literature Crusade, 1955.

———. *If.* Fort Washington, Pa.: Christian Literature Crusade, 1966.

———. *Whispers of His Power.* Old Tappan, N.J.: Revell, 1985.

Chambers, Oswald. *A Place of Help.* Fort Washington, Pa.: Christian Literature Crusade, 1973.

———. *My Utmost For His Highest.* New York: Dodd, Mead and Company, 1985.

Cowman, Mrs. Charles E. *Springs in the Valley.* Grand Rapids, Mich.: Zondervan, 1988.

———. *Streams in the Desert,* vol. 1. Grand Rapids, Mich.: Zondervan, 1986.

Fénelon, François. *Spiritual Letters to Women.* Grand Rapids, Mich.: Zondervan, 1984.

Keller, Phillip. *A Shepherd's Look at Psalm 23.* Grand Rapids, Mich.: Zondervan, 1976.

Lucado, Max. *No Wonder They Call Him Savior.* Portland, Oreg.: Multnomah, 1986.

Sanders, J. Oswald. *Spiritual Leadership.* Chicago: Moody, 1974.

Wesley, Susanna. *Prayer of Susanna Wesley.* Grand Rapids, Mich.: Zondervan, 1984.

WHEN TIME ISN'T LIMITED

Carmichael, Amy. *Learning of God*. Fort Washington, Pa.: Christian Literature Crusade, 1986.

Colson, Charles. *Loving God*. Grand Rapids, Mich.: Zondervan, 1983.

Kelly, Thomas. *Testament of Devotion*. New York: Harper and Row, 1941.

Peterson, Eugene. *Run with the Horses*. Downers Grove, Ill.: InterVarsity, 1983.

Roseveare, Helen. *Living Holiness*. Minneapolis: Bethany, 1987.

FAMILY

Arp, Dave, and Arp, Claudia. *Ten Dates for Mates*. Nashville: Thomas Nelson, 1983.

Campbell, Ross. *How to Really Love Your Child*. New York: NAL, 1982.

———. *How to Really Love Your Teenager*. Wheaton, Ill.: Victor Books, 1982.

Curran, Dolores. *Traits of a Healthy Family*. New York: Ballantine, 1984.

Dobson, James. *Dare to Discipline*. Wheaton, Ill.: Tyndale, 1973.

Elkind, David. *The Hurried Child: Growing Up Too Fast Too Soon*. Reading, Mass.: Addison-Wesley, 1981.

———. *All Grown Up and No Place to Go*. Reading, Mass.: Addison-Wesley, 1984.

Mason, Mike. *The Mystery of Marriage*. Portland, Oreg.: Multnomah, 1985.

Smalley, Gary, and Trent, John. *The Blessing*. Nashville: Thomas Nelson, 1986.

Wangerin, Walter. *As for Me and My House*. Nashville: Thomas Nelson, 1988.

GENERAL STRETCHERS

Backus, William, and Chapian, Marie. *Telling Yourself the Truth*. Minneapolis: Bethany, 1980.

Carlson, Dwight L. *Overcoming Hurts and Angers*. Eugene, Oreg.: Harvest House, 1981.

Cook, Jerry, and Baldwin, Stanley. *Love, Acceptance, and Forgiveness*. Ventura, Calif.: Regal, 1979.

Crabb, Larry. *Inside Out*. Colorado Springs, Colo.: NavPress, 1988.

Inrig, Gary. *Quality Friendship*. Chicago: Moody, 1981.

Kendall, R. T. *God Meant It for Good*. Wheaton, Ill.: Tyndale, 1988.

Lewis, C. S. *Letters to an American Lady*. Grand Rapids, Mich.: Eerdmans, 1967.

Lindbergh, Anne Morrow. *Gift from the Sea*. New York: Pantheon, 1955.

Manning, Brennan. *The Lion and the Lamb: The Relentless Tenderness of Jesus*. Old Tappan, N.J.: Revell, 1986.

Marshall, Megan. *The Cost of Loving: Women and the New Fear of Intimacy*. New York: Putnam, 1984.

McGinnis, Alan Loy. *The Friendship Factor*. Minneapolis: Augsburg, 1983.

Peck, M. Scott. *The Road Less Traveled*. New York: Simon and Schuster, 1980.

Seamands, David. *Healing Grace*. Wheaton, Ill.: Victor Books, 1988.

Thielicke, Helmut. *The Waiting Father*. New York: Harper and Row, 1981.

STRENGTHENERS FOR TIMES OF SUFFERING

Archer, Norman. *David, When Only the Grace of God Will Do.* Burlington, Ontario, Canada: Welch, 1984.

Carmichael, Amy. *Gold by Moonlight.* Fort Washington, Pa.: Christian Literature Crusade, 1960.

———. *Rose from Brier.* Fort Washington, Pa.: Christian Literature Crusade, 1972.

Wolterstorff, Nicholas. *Lament for a Son.* Grand Rapids, Mich.: Eerdmans, 1987.

RESOURCE BOOKS FOR THOSE WHO MINISTER

Beattie, Melody. *Codependent No More: How to Stop Controlling Others and Start Caring for Yourself.* Center City, Minn.: Hazelden Foundation, 1987.

Black, Claudia. *It Will Never Happen to Me!* New York: Ballantine, 1987. For children of alcoholics.

Huggett, Joyce. *Marriage on the Mend: The Power of God's Healing Love.* Downers Grove, Ill.: InterVarsity, 1988.

Keirsey, David, and Bates, Marilyn. *Please Understand Me.* Delmar, Calif.: Prometheus Nemesis, 1978. On temperaments.

Koons, Carolyn. *Beyond Betrayal.* New York: Harper and Row, 1987. For those who have had traumatic childhoods.

O'Brien, Bev. *"Mom . . . I'm Pregnant."* Wheaton, Ill.: Tyndale House, 1982. On premarital pregnancy.

Olson, Esther L., and Petersen, Kenneth. *No Place to Hide.* Wheaton, Ill.: Tyndale, 1982. On wife abuse.

Oswald, Roy M., and Kroeger, Otto. *Personality Types and Religious Leadership.* Washington, D. C.: Alban Institute, 1988. On temperaments.

Payne, Leanne. *The Broken Image.* Westchester, Ill.: Good News, 1981. On homosexuality.

Ricks, Chip. *Carol's Story.* Wheaton, Ill.: Tyndale, 1981. Anonymous true story about incest.

Seamands, David A. *Healing for Damaged Emotions.* Wheaton, Ill.: Victor, 1981.

———. *Putting Away Childish Things.* Wheaton, Ill.: Victor, 1982.

Robertson, Nan. *Getting Better.* New York: Morrow, 1988. Why AA helps so many people.

Vredevelt, Whitman. *Walking a Thin Line.* Portland, Oreg.: Multnomah, 1985. On bulimia and anorexia.

Ward, Ruth M. *Self-Esteem, Gift from God.* Grand Rapids, Mich.: Baker, 1984.

Watson, Earl. *A Silence to Be Broken.* Portland, Oreg.: Multnomah, 1986. On incest.

Williams, Pat, and Williams, Jill. *Rekindled.* Old Tappan, N.J.: Revell, 1985. On marital healing.

Woititz, Janet G. *Adult Children of Alcoholics.* Deerfield Beach, Fla.: Health Communications, 1983.

A more extensive bibliography may be found in my book *High Call, High Privilege* (Tyndale, 1981).